LIVES IN WRITING

ESSAYS

David Lodge

LIVES IN WRITING

ESSAYS

Harvill *Secker*

LONDON

Published by Harvill Secker 2014

2 4 6 8 10 9 7 5 3 1

Extracts from unpublished letters of Malcolm Bradbury are
reproduced with permission of Curtis Brown, London on behalf
of the Estate of Malcolm Bradbury

Extract from 'Letter and Date' taken from *Selected Letters* © Estate of Philip
Larkin and reprinted by permission of Faber and Faber Ltd

Extract from 'Letter to a Friend About Girls' taken from
The Complete Poems © Estate of Philip Larkin and reprinted
by permission of Faber and Faber Ltd

First published in Great Britain in 2014 by
HARVILL SECKER
Random House
20 Vauxhall Bridge Road
London SW1V 2SA

www.vintage-books.co.uk

Addresses for companies within The Random House Group Limited can be
found at:
www.randomhouse.co.uk/offices

The Random House Group Limited Reg. No. 954009

A CIP catalogue record for this book
is available from the British Library

ISBN 9781846557903 (hardback)

The Random House Group Limited supports the Forest
Stewardship Council® (FSC®), the leading international forest-
certification organisation. Our books carrying the FSC label are
printed on FSC®-certified paper. FSC is the only forest-certification scheme
supported by the leading environmental organisations,
including Greenpeace. Our paper procurement policy can be found at
www.randomhouse.co.uk/environment

Typeset in Bembo by Palimpsest Book Production Limited,
Falkirk, Stirlingshire
Printed and bound in Great Britain by Clays Ltd, St Ives PLC

To Angela, and in memory of Tom

CONTENTS

FOREWORD

I HAVE COMBINED CREATIVE writing with the practice of literary criticism for more than fifty years, and I think of myself as primarily a novelist in the former capacity, and a critic and theorist of the novel in the latter. But as I get older I find myself becoming more and more interested in, and attracted to, fact-based writing. This is I believe a common tendency in readers as they age, but it also seems to be a trend in contemporary literary culture generally. These essays variously describe, evaluate and exemplify different ways in which the lives of real people are represented in the written word: biography, the biographical novel, biographical criticism, autobiography, diary, memoir, confession, and various combinations of these modes. The book's title has another meaning: with a single exception, all the subjects are or were by profession 'in writing' of various kinds (though one of them is primarily a film-maker). The connections between their personal lives and the work they produced make a thread that runs through all these essays. Nearly all contain autobiographical passages of my own, and some in the latter part of the book are framed as memoirs. The last essay belongs to a sub-species of autobiography, of which Henry James was the supreme exponent, in which a writer tells the story behind the story of one of his books: the history of its genesis and composition, and sometimes its reception. In the title essay of an earlier book, *The Year of Henry James*, I treated my novel *Author, Author* in this way. 'Writing H.G. Wells' is more polemical. Given the controversial status of the biographical novel at the time *A Man of Parts* was published, an account of how it was written inevitably became a kind of defence of this hybrid genre.

Although I hope scholars may find things of interest in this book, it is designed primarily for the 'general reader'. In the interest of readability I have kept footnotes and bibliographical information to a minimum. Books discussed or quoted are identified simply by author, title and date of first publication.

D.L., February 2013

THE LATE GRAHAM GREENE

Norman Sherry's three-volume biography of Graham Greene* occupied him continuously and exclusively for twenty-eight years, which may be a record of some kind. Greene died in 1991, having correctly predicted that he would not live to read the second volume, which was published in 1994. He also prophesied that Sherry would not survive to read the third and last volume, eventually published in 2004, a remark in which one might detect some resentment at the ever-increasing scale and scope of the biography, and regret for having authorised its often embarrassing revelations. That prophecy was happily unfulfilled, but at times it was a close-run thing. Sherry promised Greene that he would visit every country that the novelist had used as a setting for a novel, a vow that took him to some twenty countries, entailing danger, hardship, and at least one life-threatening illness. He admits on the penultimate page of the biography that 'reaching the end had often seemed beyond my strength and spirit', and superstitiously left the very last sentence of his narrative unfinished.

It is impossible not to see in the progress of this

---

* *The Life of Graham Greene, Volume One 1904–1939* (1989); *Volume Two 1939–1955* (1994); *Volume Three 1955–1991* (2004).

enormous work a cautionary tale about the perils of
literary biography when it becomes an obsessive and
all-consuming project, a doomed attempt to re-live the
subject's life vicariously and somehow achieve a perfect
'fit' between it and his artistic output. 'No novel can be
believable if the novelist does not acknowledge the truth
of his own experiences, even when these are disturbing,'
Sherry asserts in the course of this final instalment.
'Greene needed to deal with his past: and we, in turn,
need to excavate his private history.' There are several
debatable assertions here. What does 'truth' mean in this
context? If we grant that writers often deal with painful
and disturbing personal experience in their fictions (and
Greene himself wrote that 'writing is a form of therapy')
does this not usually involve departing from the empirical
facts of such experience — altering them, even inverting
them, reinterpreting them, and combining them with
purely fictional material? If so, is there not a danger in
trying to pin down the sources of characters and events
of novels too literally in the writer's own life? Does a
novel become more 'believable' when we succeed in
doing this? Or less?

These questions belong to a larger debate which has
exercised literary critics and scholars since T.S. Eliot
declared in 1919 that 'the more perfect the artist, the
more completely separate in him will be the man who
suffers and the mind which creates; the more perfectly
will the mind digest and transmute the passions which
are its material'. Eliot challenged the Romantic view
that the creative process is essentially expressive of the
writer's self, and by implication the legitimacy of
biographical interpretation, contributing crucially to the

emergence of a new movement in academic literary criticism which regarded the text as an autonomous verbal object, and by the end of the twentieth century had triumphantly affirmed the 'death of the author'. Meanwhile non-academic readers showed an increasing interest in biographies of authors, which were often written by academics of an empirical and historical bent. The fact is that the appeal of literary biography is undeniable and irresistible but cognitively impure. We are fascinated by the mystery of literary creation, and therefore eager to discover the sources of a writer's inspiration; but we also take a simply inquisitive human interest in the private lives of important writers, especially if they involve behaviour that is in any way unusual. Graham Greene was a man whose life offered ample opportunity to satisfy both kinds of curiosity – perhaps so much opportunity that Norman Sherry allowed himself to be overwhelmed and in the end exhausted by it.

His first volume, covering the years 1904–39, was by far the best, convincingly locating the source of Greene's obsession with the theme of treachery in his unhappy childhood, and telling vividly and lucidly the absorbing story of his up-and-down early career as a writer, and his remarkable courtship, marriage and extra-marital sexual life. It thoroughly deserved the praise it attracted. The second volume was less satisfying, because its thematic organisation obscured the narrative line of Greene's life in the period 1939–55, but it did memorably contain the stranger-than-fiction story of Greene's love affair with Catherine Walston, wife of the British Labour politician Harry Walston, which

inspired *The End of the Affair* (dedicated 'To C.'). The
third volume, at 900 pages, is the longest and also the
weakest. Sherry's determination to find a real-life model
for every important character in Greene's novels,
unweaving their artful blend of observed fact and imaginative invention, becomes increasingly obtrusive, and in
spite of the book's enormous length and plethora of
facts, there are puzzling gaps. If there was a reference
to *Dr Fischer of Geneva* (1980), for instance, I missed
it, and there is none in the index. This enigmatic fable
was a minor work, but one would like to know something about the background to its composition and its
reception. Was it passed over because it had no obvious
source in Greene's life?

Apart from what we learn from Greene's letters,
which are quoted at length, we get from this book a
less vivid sense of what Greene was actually like as a
person in later life than from the much shorter and more
selective memoirs of the companion of his later years,
Yvonne Cloetta, and his friend Shirley Hazzard.* Sherry
has no anecdote as revealing as, for instance, Yvonne
Cloetta's first intimation of *The Honorary Consul*:

> One morning, he appeared in the doorway,
> looking extremely worried, and announced quite
> abruptly, 'It's terrible to think that from now on
> I'm going to have to live for three years with a
> certain Charlie Fortnum.' And he went back to

* Yvonne Cloetta, *In Search of a Beginning: My Life with Graham
Greene*, as told to Marie-Françoise Allain (2004); Shirley Hazzard,
Greene on Capri: A Memoir (2000).

whatever he was doing, without saying another word.

Greene knew from experience how long a full-length novel would take to complete at this stage of his life, and how much it would cost him. 'Retirement is always a distressing time for a man. But for a writer it is death,' he remarked to Yvonne Cloetta on another occasion. So he went on writing although he found it harder and harder, and was seldom satisfied with what he produced, even when his readers were. He was his own harshest critic. 'I think it stinks,' he said, sending the manuscript of *Our Man in Havana* to Catherine; and of *A Burnt-Out Case*, again to Catherine: 'I hate the book. There are bits I like, but I've hardly had a moment of pleasure working this time and the result is muddled and shapeless.' His well-known practice of writing a certain number of words a day (500, later reduced to 300) was a ritual that enabled him to carry on a task that he often found agonisingly difficult. The gradual accumulation of words was reassuring and he attributed to the figures an almost magical significance, cabling Catherine on the completion of *A Burnt-Out Case*: 'FINISHED THANK GOD 325 WORDS SHORT ORIGINAL ESTIMATE.' The novelist Shirley Hazzard was friendly with Greene from the late 1960s onwards, when she and her husband lived on Capri where Greene had a villa. 'When from time to time Graham told us, "I have a book coming out," he would occasionally add, "Not a specially good one."' Hazzard's own summary judgement of the later work cannot be bettered:

The inspired pain of the earlier fiction would not recur; or even the intensity of those lighter and livelier works that Graham had once differentiated as 'entertainments.' What remained was professionalism: a unique view and tone, a practised, topical narrative that held the interest and forced the pace of the reader. Poignancy was largely subsumed into world-weariness, resurfacing in spasms of authenticity.

The final instalment of Sherry's biography is then – perhaps inevitably, given Greene's long productive life – a story of gradual decline of creative power from a very high peak of achievement. The second volume ended with the composition of *The Quiet American* (1955), Greene's last fully achieved masterpiece. It was also the first novel to hint at the waning of his belief in the Roman Catholic religious doctrine which had underpinned his most powerful and important previous novels, from *Brighton Rock* (1938) to *The End of the Affair* (1951). Politics, rather than religion, provides the ideological frame of reference which defines character and conflict in *The Quiet American*, and it has acquired a justified reputation as a novel prophetic not only of the folly of the American involvement in Vietnam but also of other ill-fated foreign adventures, including the war in Iraq. Greene's play *The Potting Shed*, a hit in London in 1957, but a flop in New York, showed that his imagination was still kindled by the more extreme paradoxes of Catholic spirituality, but *Our Man in Havana* (1958) treated potentially dark and serious matter in a spirit of comedy. This was a time of great turmoil in Greene's personal life. His grand passion for Catherine Walston was slowly and painfully burning itself out. Though they continued to meet occasionally, Catherine resisted Greene's pleas to leave her husband and children to live with him – in exactly what terms, we don't know, because he burned all her letters; but his letters to her have survived and Sherry quotes them extensively. Greene was now in love with another woman, the Swedish actress Anita Björk, whose husband had recently committed suicide. He visited her frequently in Stockholm, and there was evidently a strong sexual charge between them, but Anita, tied to her career and her children, was no more willing than Catherine to throw in her lot with him. Could this, one wonders, have been the secret attraction of both relationships for Greene, always shy of emotional ties and commitments, even as he agonised over them? (*The Human Factor* has an epigraph from Conrad: 'I only know that he who forms a tie is lost.') He refers openly to his assignations with Anita in his letters to Catherine, perhaps as a subtle form of punishment, but he never wants to break off either relationship. After parting from, and then returning to, Anita, he writes to Catherine: 'I feel hopelessly muddled. I missed her more than I thought I would, but now that's healed, it's you I miss. Am I crazy or do I just happen to love two women as I never have before?' Several people thought he *was* crazy, including his wife Vivien, who cited his compulsive travelling, never staying in one place for more than a few weeks. There is probably enough material for a book called *Graham Greene, Frequent Flyer*. At the end of one year he calculated that he had flown more than 40,000 miles, quite a lot for someone whose occupation is usually described as 'sedentary'. His letters to Catherine constantly proposed meetings in various exotic locations all round the globe; and his friend Michael Meyer tells an amusing story of an exhausting trip to Fiji and Tahiti that Greene arranged simply to escape Christmas, a feast he did not enjoy. Because of problems with their flights and weather they crossed the international dateline three times and experienced three successive Christmas Eves.

Greene was still married to Vivien, though living apart from her, and he never sought a divorce, annulment, or legal separation. In the eyes of the Church he was of course committing grave sin. He had his own way of reconciling his conduct with his conscience – or perhaps by the late 1950s he had privately ceased to believe in the validity of Catholic moral theology. To the world at large, though, he was still the great Catholic Novelist (however strenuously he insisted that he was a novelist who happened to be a Catholic) and the experience of being pestered and appealed to for spiritual guidance by various devout and often troubled co-religionists, including priests, was an irony that caused him much embarrassment. 'I felt myself used and exhausted by the victims of religion . . .' he complained later. 'I was like a man without medical knowledge in a village struck with plague.' When the affair with Anita finally came to an end in 1958, Greene's appeals to Catherine became more fervent, and his frustration more acute. He was also oppressed by the fear that his creativity was drying up. According to Sherry he came near to suicide, not for the first time in his life. Instead he went to a leper colony in the Congo, seeking material for a new novel.

A Burnt-Out Case (1961) is not a completely satisfactory novel, but it is a peculiarly fascinating one for anyone interested in Greene because of its confessional nature. In the character of Querry, the famous Catholic architect who is praised as much for his spirituality as his artistry, but who in fact reveals himself to be totally lacking in faith in either art or religion, and a cold-hearted failure in personal relationships, Greene deliberately invited a biographical reading of the novel that would be uncomfortable for his Catholic admirers. Sherry, needless to say, finds models for other characters, and without much difficulty, since Greene was more or less making up the story as he did his research, putting in characters and incidents that he observed, as one can see from his journal written at the time, later published in *In Search of a Character: two African Journals* (1961). But Sherry's effort to connect the character of the obnoxious journalist Parkinson with a friend of Greene's called Ronald Matthews seems to me forced and unconvincing. Matthews was a journalist who had written a memoir of Greene, published in French as *Mon Ami Graham Greene*, which Greene disliked enough to prevent its publication in English; but there is no significant resemblance between the two men. What makes Parkinson live as a character, as Sherry's quotations from the novel remind us, is Greene's creative use of language, first, in describing the journalist's gross physical appearance ('his neck as he lay on his bed was forced into three ridges like gutters, and the sweat filled them and drained round the curve of his head on to the pillow'), and secondly in the wonderfully cynical rhetoric with which Parkinson defends his sensationally fabricated journalism, e.g.: 'Do

you really believe Caesar said *Et tu, Brute?* It's what he
ought to have said and someone . . . spotted what was
needed. The truth is always forgotten.'

During this trip Greene made the acquaintance of
a French couple, Jacques and Yvonne Cloetta, and
Yvonne probably contributed something to the character
of Marie, the young wife of the *colon* Rycker in *A
Burnt-Out Case*. Some months later she returned to the
South of France with her children, leaving her husband
working in Africa, and Greene commenced an affair
with her which, rather amazingly, they managed to
conceal from Jacques for eight years, after which he
seems to have condoned it, on condition that they were
discreet. In the mid-1960s Greene made his principal
home in Antibes, where Yvonne lived, and they settled
down into a relationship which lasted until the end of
his life. During this decade Catherine's health began to
deteriorate: surgery after an accident was botched, and
Sherry thinks she became an alcoholic. Greene told her
about Yvonne, for whom he said (in a letter of 1967)
he had 'a real quiet love . . . "peaceful as old age"', in
contrast to their own 'tormented love – love which
made one more happy and sometimes more miserable
than I'll ever be again . . . I always remember that never
for a moment have I ever been bored by you – enraptured, excited, nervous, angry, tormented, but never
bored, because I lost myself in searching for you.' But
his letters became less frequent and the relationship
slowly atrophied, as Catherine became chronically ill
and they met at longer and longer intervals. She died
of leukaemia in 1978, her beauty wasted, and refused to
let Greene see her in her last illness. Harry Walston

wrote a remarkably magnanimous reply to the remorseful letter of condolence Greene apparently sent him: 'You should not have remorse. Of course you caused pain. But who can honestly say that he has gone through life without causing pain? And you gave joy too.' From then onwards Yvonne was the only woman of consequence in Greene's life.

Though Greene acquired the apartment in Antibes in 1966 in order to be near Yvonne (he already had a flat in Paris), the decision to settle permanently in France at this time was taken for quite other reasons. His financial affairs were in crisis. Greene had entrusted a great deal of his money (and his royalties must have been considerable ever since *The Heart of the Matter* became a world bestseller in 1948, not to mention the income from his plays and films) to his accountant, one Thomas Roe CBE, a well-connected and highly respected man who undertook to protect it from the high rates of British income tax by using foreign tax havens and tax-efficient investment schemes. Greene was not his only distinguished client – Noel Coward and Robert Graves also availed themselves of his services. Roe, however, turned out to be a swindler, with criminal associates and mafia connections. One of the companies he was involved in collapsed spectacularly in 1964. In 1965 he was arrested in Switzerland and charged with abuse of confidence, fraud, and passing counterfeit dollar notes. In 1968 he was convicted and sentenced to six years' imprisonment. Greene not only lost a great deal of money by Roe's perfidy – according to his good friend, the film director Peter Glenville, 'Graham, through Roe, lost *all*, repeat *all*' – he also became liable for a hefty tax bill. And according to Sherry, 'there was a chance that the British authorities, if Greene had not become domiciled in another country, and had he not been willing to pay back what he owed, might have attempted to secure his arrest'. Sherry is irritatingly vague about this matter, as he often is when you most want hard facts from him. But it is obvious that this episode caused Greene much anxiety and despondency, which, as Sherry observes, seem to be reflected in his troubled visage in the photographic portraits made by Lord Snowdon at the time. It explains a lot, too about his subsequent lifestyle. Many visitors to his Antibes apartment, myself included, were surprised by its modest scale, but at the time he bought it he was hard pressed for cash. 'I live on a shoestring and a Swiss overdraft,' he wrote to Catherine on 10 June 1966. In due course his fortunes recovered, and according to Yvonne Cloetta, when towards the end of his life he asked his lawyer for a rough estimate of his wealth he was astonished at its size. For a long time he had arranged to be paid a regular income from a company set up for the purpose. Personally he was never a big spender, and according to Shirley Hazzard he was parsimonious to the point of meanness in trivial matters, taking buses rather than taxis home from Gemma's restaurant on Capri, and being reluctant to turn up the central heating in his villa *Il Rosario* on chilly days. But he was often generous with gifts to causes and individuals. The value of his estate at death seems to be unknown, perhaps because he died in fiscally secretive Switzerland. In a footnote

Sherry quotes the *Toronto Star* (a surprising source) stating that it was only about £200,000, commenting: 'I doubt that this is the whole story, but I know he gave away vast sums to friends and family through his corporation Verdant.'

The Thomas Roe episode is one of the most interesting revelations in Sherry's third volume, because Greene's tax exile had important consequences for his literary career. His visits to England were henceforth severely restricted (he writes to Catherine in 1967 that he will receive an honorary degree in Edinburgh 'If the tax people allow!') and he gradually lost touch with, and seemingly interest in, his native country. It is a matter for regret that the acute and eloquent observation of English culture and society in the novels up to *The End of the Affair* is not to be found in the later ones. When he did set a late novel mainly in England – *The Human Factor* (1978) – his descriptive touch was not as sure as it used to be, and his social focus narrower. Nor did he write very much about his adopted country, France. Instead, the practice established by *The Quiet American*, *Our Man in Havana* and *A Burnt-Out Case* continued: he went hunting for material in exotic locations and trouble-spots: Haiti, Sinai, Northern Ireland, Russia, Argentina, Paraguay, Panama, Nicaragua. He acquired a reputation for anticipating where a political crisis would soon take place, and rather enjoyed it: 'A few days ago *The Times* reported a plot against the President & three colonels arrested – so I seem to have picked right again,' he writes gleefully to Yvonne from Paraguay in July 1968. Not all these trips produced novels, but they usually yielded a non-fiction book, or journalistic articles, or letters to the press.

In later life Greene frequently used his status and celebrity to intervene in international politics. Sometimes this was entirely to his credit, as when he gave support to the Soviet dissident writers Sinyavsky and Daniel in 1967 by publicly requesting that his blocked Russian royalties should be paid to their wives, because he had no desire to revisit the country as long as they languished in prison; but he went on to say that this should not be taken as a criticism of the Soviet Union, where he would choose to live in preference to America. Commentators were quick to point out that in such a case it would not be long before he shared the fate of Sinyavsky and Daniel. Greene's political gestures were seldom free from paradox, inconsistency or internal contradiction. The often-quoted statement in his 1969 Shakespeare Prize acceptance speech, 'The writer should always be ready to change sides at the drop of a hat. He speaks up for the victims, and the victims change', is not the all-accommodating loophole he claimed it to be. At about the same time as the Sinyavsky–Daniel affair, he gave considerable offence in Britain by writing an admiring introduction to the autobiography of his old Secret Service colleague, the traitor Kim Philby. Greene wrote: 'He betrayed his country – yes, perhaps he did, but who among us has not committed treason to something or someone more important than a country?' This is pure sophistry, because 'country' in this context was not an abstraction but a human community, including many British agents whom Philby sent to certain death. Sherry recalls that when he pressed Greene to condemn those deeds of Philby, he uncharacteristically became red with anger, and refused to do so.

Greene kept his word and did not return to Russia until 1987, when he participated in a peace conference convened under the regime of Gorbachev, whom he admired and wished to support. He made a speech improbably celebrating an alliance between Catholics and Communists. 'We are fighting together against the death squads in El Salvador. We are fighting together against the Contras in Nicaragua. We are fighting together against General Pinochet in Chile. There is no division in our thoughts between Roman Catholics and Communists.' This rhetoric blatantly ignored a division within the clergy and laity of the Roman Catholic Church, between conservatives who often supported oppressive right-wing regimes, and those on the political left influenced by liberation theology. Greene's tendency to support any Latin American political movement that was ideologically leftist and hostile to the USA often led him into an uncritical alliance with politicians who were as ruthless in their methods as those they opposed. Sherry has done his homework in this area, and even if he tells you more than you really want to know about the political history of Cuba, Haiti, Panama and the rest, he does enable an informed assessment of Greene's treatment of these matters in his novels and reportage.

Describing the novelist's surprisingly warm friendship with the populist leader of Panama, General Omar Torrijos, in the five years preceding his death in a suspicious air crash in 1981, Sherry observes that 'as Greene got older he seemed to take more risks, made up his mind in favour of those leading dangerous lives'. One might also cite his fascination with guerrillas and revolutionaries in books like *The Comedians* and *The Honorary Consul* (probably the best of the late novels). But one must bear in mind that all this time he was regularly reporting on his travels to the British Secret Service. Sherry adds little to what he revealed in the second volume about this topic, but Yvonne Cloetta is unequivocal in conversation with Marie-Françoise Allain: 'What I can tell you is that, to the very end, he worked with the British Services.'

This puts Greene's provocative public support for revolutionary struggle in a rather different perspective. It also raises a question which Sherry largely ignores: Greene's attitude to British politics. In his second volume Sherry reported in a footnote that Greene voted Conservative in the general election of 1945 – 'the socialists are such bores,' he told his mother in explanation – a rather extraordinary fact when one considers that almost everybody in the country of even mildly progressive views voted Labour on that occasion. In the third volume we learn that Greene confessed to Catherine, whose husband was a Labour parliamentary candidate, that he celebrated the defeat of that party under Hugh Gaitskell in 1959 with a slug of whisky while in a plane over Canada. Yvonne Cloetta recalls that he was delighted by Mrs Thatcher's victory in 1979, explaining, when she expressed surprise, 'It doesn't make a great difference with us, Labour or Conservative, in day-to-day life, or even in politics, but I'm pleased mainly because, for once, it's a woman.' It's difficult to reconcile these laid-back attitudes to British politics with those Greene struck on the international stage. I have not changed the opinion I expressed in an earlier essay about Greene, that his interventions in politics, both public and secret, were not driven by any coherent ideological conviction, but were essentially personal, emotional, and opportunistic in motivation.

Greene's religious views are just as difficult to determine. He 'was ever in a confused state about the condition of his faith', Sherry remarks, but this was perhaps more forgivable than his political inconsistencies. Few of us, whether we define ourselves as religious believers, ex-believers, or non-believers, are completely consistent in our answers to the ultimate questions about life and death. Even convinced atheists have been known to light a candle in a church on occasion. (Tony Harrison has a fine poem on the subject.) It was Greene's fate, however, to have to act out his uncertainty on the stage of his celebrity. *A Burnt-Out Case* was an oblique announcement that he no longer believed in the letter of Catholic dogma; in due course he was more explicit in interviews, notably one with John Cornwell in the Catholic weekly, *The Tablet*, in September 1989, where he described himself as a 'Catholic agnostic'. In another interview he described himself more oxymoronically as a 'Catholic atheist'. He drew a distinction between 'belief' which he had lost, and 'faith' which he retained, though the latter always seemed to me more like a wistful kind of hope that the whole Christian myth might improbably turn out to be true.

Sherry, who describes himself as a lapsed Catholic,

suggests that in his later years Greene was edging back towards the fold. 'Greene was concerned about his promiscuity, wanted forgiveness to escape punishment in hell and be received in the arms of God.' The main evidence for this bold assertion is Greene's curious relationship with the Spanish priest Fr Leopoldo Duran, which inspired the whimsical fable *Monsignor Quixote* (1982) and which Duran himself described in his memoir, *Graham Greene: Friend and Brother* (1994). For many years Greene would spend a week or two with him in the summer, being driven about the Spanish countryside, always ending up at the monastery of Osera. On Sundays during these trips, or when staying in the flat in Antibes, Duran would say mass for the two of them, Greene told Cornwell – adding ambiguously: 'And to please Fr Duran I make a confession now.' In his memoir, Duran describes how he was summoned by Greene to his deathbed and administered the last sacraments, and asserts that Greene died a fully reconciled member of the Church. Yvonne Cloetta, however, gives a rather different spin to the episode: 'I had indeed suggested summoning his friend, the Spanish priest, Leopoldo Duran. He raised his hand casually and said, "Oh, if you want to . . ." That implied he was indifferent.' Sherry himself did not arrive on the scene until after Greene's death, and the details of the writer's last days and hours are incomplete. In this respect as in so many others, this enigmatic man carried his secrets to the grave.

Graham Greene's career as an author mostly predated our modern publicity-driven literary world of book tours, literary festivals and gladiatorial prize competitions, and in later years, apart from giving an increasing number of press interviews, he generally kept clear of it. Towards the end of his life, however, he did get involved in one very typical manifestation of this new literary culture. In 1989 the Guinness Peat Aviation Company founded a prize worth a record 50,000 Irish punts for the best book written by an Irishman or established resident in Ireland in the last three years, and invited Greene to choose the winner from a shortlist to be drawn up by a panel of distinguished judges, who laboured for many months sifting the works submitted. Greene, however, sought to overrule the judges and award the prize to a book not on the shortlist, *The Broken Commandment* by Vincent McDonnell, which he himself had helped to get published after it had been sent to him in manuscript by McDonnell's wife. This caused huge consternation, anger and embarrassment, and the crisis was only resolved by giving a special prize (in fact funded out of Greene's pocket) of 20,000 punts to McDonnell, while John Banville received the main prize for *The Book of Evidence*, but the controversy and recriminations continued for some time. It was a tragi-comic episode which took its toll on Greene and may have hastened his death (which like Catherine's was caused by leukaemia). 'Dublin killed me,' he said to Sherry later. Sherry argues plausibly that Greene adopted McDonnell as a kind of literary son and channelled into his cause some of the emotion generated by his own failure to win the Nobel Prize for Literature. He was denied this accolade year after year, partly because of the implacable hostility of one Swedish Academician, Arthur Lundkvist, but also because

other members of the academy thought he was more
of an 'entertainer' than a 'serious' writer. That was a grave
misjudgement. It is true that Greene used throughout
his career the structures of the adventure stories he read
in his childhood and youth, which accounted in part
for his wide readership. But he combined his page-
turning narrative technique with a unique and unsettling
vision of the world which subverted and transformed
the stereotypes of popular fiction. He was also a master
of English prose (something which Scandinavian readers
are perhaps not able fully to appreciate).

The same, alas, cannot be said for his biographer.
Sherry's third volume is self-indulgently and often eccen-
trically written. The discourse is frequently broken up
into short sections consisting of a paragraph or two,
separated by asterisks, which disrupt the cohesion of the
narrative and afford the biographer too much freedom
for digression and superfluous comment. Mixed meta-
phors run amok (e.g., 'When Greene writes a letter to
the press, it's a lightning rod for shoals of letters to be
poured out in answer, swords drawn.'). Similes often
baffle (e.g., 'Had he failed this couple [the McDonnells],
he'd have been as ashamed as a nudist caught with his
clothes on.'). Sometimes, like Nabokov's Kinbote in *Pale
Fire*, Sherry addresses the startled reader directly: 'Don't
you feel that at times, writing a novel was for him a
disease?' Towards the end of the book there are lurid
disquisitions on the horror of death which seem to tell
us more about the biographer than his subject. Either
Sherry was poorly served by his editors or he ignored
their advice. This is a great pity, because his dedication
to his task is manifest, and the research that has gone

into the book is awe-inspiring. With all its faults the completed biography is an indispensable companion to the work of a major modern writer, and a fascinating account of an extraordinary life.

THE RISE AND FALL AND RISE AND FALL
OF KINGSLEY AMIS

Z ACHARY LEADER'S BIOGRAPHY of Kingsley Amis*
runs to more than 1,000 pages, including ninety-
seven pages of notes, many of them substantial. Did its
subject deserve this enormous biographical effort and
corresponding demand on the reader's time? Answers to
that question would depend very much on the respond-
ent's age and nationality. For English readers and writers
born in the 1930s (like myself) or a little before, Kingsley
Amis was a key figure in post-war British culture, whose
importance and influence cannot be measured simply by
the intrinsic merit of his books. In America he acquired
a small band of fans, mostly Anglophile academics, but
the wider reading public never really embraced him with
any warmth. *Lucky Jim*, a critically acclaimed bestseller
in the UK, sold only 2,000 copies in the US in its first
two years. According to Zachary Leader, it was not until
Edmund Wilson reviewed Amis's second novel, *That
Uncertain Feeling*, in *The New Yorker* in 1956, comparing
him to Evelyn Waugh, that he began to be taken seriously
in America, and even so, Leader observes, 'Amis never
sold well there.' Leader says nothing about translations

* *The Life of Kingsley Amis* (2006).

and foreign sales of his work, but my impression is that Amis's fiction, like warm English beer, is a taste that Continental Europe never acquired.

Why was this so? It was, I believe, because Amis's distinctive and original attitudes to literary tradition, to class, to morals and manners, were mediated in a style, a tone of voice, the expressiveness of which was fully appreciated only within his own English speech community. With his friend Philip Larkin, of whom the same might be said, Amis led a consciously insular movement in English writing in the 1950s, sometimes unhelpfully called 'the Movement' and sometimes conflated with the more journalistic concept of the Angry Young Men. Amis publicly disowned these labels, but he was well aware of the new trend in English writing in the 1950s which they designated and his own crucial role in it. In aesthetic terms it was anti-modernist – a very different category from postmodernist – being conservative as regards literary form. Amis and his associates challenged the cultural prestige of high modernism (Joyce, Pound, Eliot, Woolf, *et al.*) and deplored its continuing influence on English poetry and literary fiction. In their criticism and by example they opposed experimentalism, obscurity, exiguous plots, exotic settings, and borrowings from what Philip Larkin derisively called 'the myth kitty'. They wrote about ordinary blokes (they themselves were mostly male) having ordinary experiences in ordinary places, like English provincial towns and redbrick universities. They voiced the feelings of a new generation of lower-middle-class youth pushed up the social ladder by free secondary and tertiary education in post-war Britain, who felt to some extent alienated from their roots but also resented and resisted the assumptions and prejudices of the established professional class into which they had been promoted. *Lucky Jim* struck a nerve in this generation, a nerve of delighted recognition and vicarious wish-fulfilment, but what made it stand out was Amis's prose style, which may be represented by Jim Dixon's famous reflection on the title of his scholarly article, '*The Economic Influence of the Developments in Shipbuilding Techniques, 1450 to 1485*':

> Dixon had read, or begun to read, dozens like it, but his own seemed worse than most in its air of being convinced of its own usefulness and significance. 'In considering this strangely neglected topic,' it began. *This what neglected topic? This strangely what topic? This strangely neglected what?*

John Lewis, the narrator of *That Uncertain Feeling*, describes returning home after an amorous extra-marital encounter in the same style:

> Feeling a tremendous rakehell, and not liking myself much for it, and feeling rather a good chap for not liking myself much for it, and not liking myself at all for feeling rather a good chap, I got indoors, vigorously rubbing lipstick off my mouth with my handkerchief.

Essentially this is prose that puts truthfulness before elegance, especially 'elegant variation', but manages to achieve a kind of eloquence as well as humour with lexical and syntactical repetition that seems superficially clumsy. The aim is always to be honest, exact, and undeceived. It was a style that Amis had cultivated and honed in correspondence with Larkin long before either of them was published, and it helped a lot of other young British writers to find their own voices.

Amis's place as leader and trend-setter did not last for much more than a decade. Society changed, literary fashion changed, and he changed. But he remained a significant figure in English letters, maintaining throughout his life a prolific output, not only of novels (twenty-five in all) but also numerous non-fiction books of various kinds, television screenplays, a vast amount of journalism, and a significant number of poems that have stood the test of time. He enjoyed his celebrity, and used his access to the media to comment on social and political issues of the day, as his views swung from left to right in the course of his life. That his son Martin achieved comparable fame and influence among his generation caused Amis *père* some irritation as well as pride, but helped to maintain his own prominent position in English cultural life. His personal life was also full of interest, with fascinating links to his work, and is well documented. In short, he fully deserved a major biography.

Amis's own *Memoirs*, published in 1991, though entertaining and occasionally revealing, was not an autobiography but a collection of discontinuous reminiscences, character-sketches and reflections that gave away little about the writer's private and emotional life. It was also, according to several disgruntled people described in its pages, factually unreliable. Not long

afterwards Amis approved and to some extent assisted
a biography of himself written by Eric Jacobs, a journalist and fellow habitué of the Garrick Club. Published
in the spring of 1995, it revealed a very different person
behind Amis's bluff, blimpish and entertaining public
mask: someone who for most of his life had been
subject to anxiety, panic attacks, and various phobias,
who would not fly, drive, or travel on the Underground,
and was dependent on other people to manage the
simplest tasks of life. It was an eye-opening book for
those interested in the subject's personal history, but
under-researched and inadequate in its treatment of
Amis the writer. When it was finished Jacobs obtained
Kingsley's agreement to record their conversations in
the manner of a latter-day Boswell, with a view to
eventual publication. There was also an informal understanding that Jacobs would in due course edit Amis's
letters.

By this time Amis was in poor health, and drinking
heavily, as he had been for years. In the autumn of 1995
he had a serious fall and after a few weeks of illness
and dementia, very distressing to his family, he died
peacefully in his sleep on 22 October. With extraordinary tactlessness, Jacobs attempted to rush into print
with his observations of Amis's last weeks of life, and
approached some newspapers with the material. When
Martin Amis protested, Jacobs immediately backed
down, but he was not invited to the funeral, and the
editorship of the letters was given to Zachary Leader,
a friend of Martin's. This was perhaps hard luck for
Jacobs (who died in 2003), but fortunate for readers of
Kingsley Amis. Leader is an academic critic with a

special interest in modern British writing. American by birth, he has lived the larger part of his adult life in England, long enough to respond to the nuances of Amis's prose. His monumental, meticulously annotated edition of Amis's *Letters*, published in 2000, did full justice to the richness of the material, for Amis was one of the great letter-writers of the twentieth century, and certainly one of the funniest. His early correspondence with Philip Larkin, whose *Selected Letters* edited by Anthony Thwaite (1992) displayed an equally expressive epistolary style, is a fascinating record of the formation of the literary ideas and practices that eventually flowered in the Movement. Simultaneously with the Amis *Letters*, Martin Amis published *Experience*, a complex memoir of an extraordinary concatenation of events in his life in 1995, including his father's last illness and death, and containing many vivid anecdotes of their relationship from childhood onwards. Leader draws on these sources, but also provides a great deal of information that is new, recovered from unpublished manuscript material and from wide-ranging interviews with people who knew Amis. Many of the latter were hurt by him, in print or in life. There was an aggressive streak in his character, and he derived a devilish glee from flaunting rudeness and prejudice which tested his friends' and family's tolerance to the limit. 'Few writers have written as perceptively about bad behaviour as Amis or been as consistently accused of it,' Leader observes. He achieves the feat – especially difficult for any 'authorised' biographer – of being both empathetic with and critical of his subject. Reading this book one is at various points surprised, amused, fascinated and shocked, but one closes it at the end impressed by the ruthless honesty with which Kingsley Amis explored and confronted the less amiable aspects of his own character in his imaginative writing.

As a narrative, it has a wave-like structure, and might have been called *The Rise and Fall and Rise and Fall of Kingsley Amis*, the two crests of his literary career being the successes of *Lucky Jim* and *The Old Devils* (with which he won the Booker Prize in 1986). In the trough between these two books there was much personal unhappiness, angst, accidie, and ill-health, from which he seemed to recover for a period before a final descent into dissolution and death, the fear of which had always haunted him, as it did Philip Larkin.

'Kingsley Amis' is a good name for a writer – both parts of it being unusual and instantly memorable. His given name probably derives from the popular Victorian novelist Charles Kingsley, but it is not likely that Amis's parents had such a vocation in mind for their son when they named him after a cousin of his mother's. Born in 1922, he was their only child – according to family rumour the birth was so traumatic that conjugal relations subsequently ceased. Mrs Amis was certainly panicked by any allusion to sex in the home – Amis recalled a 'fierce (and absurdly visible) shake of the head' at the mention in his presence when he was about fourteen of 'somebody's honeymoon or some such depravity'. The family was lower-middle-class, its ethos a genteel secularised Protestantism. Mr Amis was employed as a clerk with a firm in the City of London, and Mrs Amis was a housewife. They occupied a series of modest houses in a nondescript suburb called Norbury on the southern rim of Greater London. What saved Amis from a childhood of crippling dullness was the City of London School where his father enrolled him at the age of twelve and where he was supported after one year by a scholarship. This was by all accounts, including Amis's, an admirable institution which modelled itself on public schools but took its pupils from a wider social range and, being a day school, did not cut them off from normal life during term. In 1939, however, when the outbreak of war seemed inevitable, the school was evacuated to share the teaching facilities of Marlborough, a traditional boarding school, and so Amis came to experience the kind of educational ambience that he had previously known only vicariously from juvenile reading.

It was virtually an all-male environment, as were St John's College, Oxford, where he went in 1941 to begin reading English, and the army into which he was called up in 1942, interrupting his studies for the duration of the war. So from his late adolescence into early adulthood girls were scarce and seldom sexually available, and his closest personal relationships were with other young men, notably with Philip Larkin, who was already at St John's, and also reading English, when Amis went up to Oxford. Larkin had a similar social background to Amis's, and they had the same tastes in literature, jazz, and humour. They immediately became fast friends. 'It was love, unquestionably love on my father's part,' Martin commented in *Experience*, after reading Amis's early letters to Larkin, an intense feeling of affinity which the former both acknowledged and defused by referring to the latter occasionally as 'dalling'. From an unpublished and uncompleted novel called 'Who Else Is Rank?' which Amis wrote in collaboration with a fellow officer during his military service, and a short story by Philip Larkin called 'Seven', it is clear that there was a homosexual element in the group to which they belonged at Oxford, and a camp style was adopted by some of its heterosexual members. This may partly explain Amis's determination later to seize every possible opportunity for fornication, as if he needed to reassure himself about his own sexual identity. (In one of his letters to Elizabeth Jane Howard, with whom he fell in love in 1962, he says: 'thanks to you I have dismissed for ever any lingering doubts about my masculinity and all that.')

Amis joined the Royal Signals in 1942, correctly calculating that this would be one of the safest branches of the military in a war because its activities are usually well to the rear of any fighting. Nevertheless his unit was posted to France only three weeks after D–Day, and followed the British forces across Europe until the end of the war, so he cannot have been entirely out of danger. When I reviewed the *Letters* in the *Times Literary Supplement* I speculated that perhaps Amis's chronic anxiety and panic attacks had their origin in some concealed wartime trauma, but there is no evidence for this in Leader's detailed account of his military service. Nor, either in his letters or published comments, does Amis seem to have had any sense of taking part in the climactic chapter of an historical epic. The short stories he wrote about the army and the

relevant chapters of 'Who Else Is Rank' focus on regi-
mental life as a microcosm of British civil society, and
the prospects of change in this realm in the future. In
his first years as an undergraduate at Oxford Amis, like
many of his contemporaries, including Iris Murdoch,
joined the communist-dominated Labour Club and
later the Communist Party itself. He described this
later in life as a form of rebellion against his father,
though it was also a way of meeting liberated girls,
one of whom relieved him of his virginity. He certainly
soon tired of earnest discussions of dialectical materialism, and the effect of his military experience was to
turn him away from dogmatic Marxism to a democratic
socialism which would allow plenty of individual
freedom. The young soldier corresponding to Amis in
'Who Else Is Rank?' dreams of a post-war England
'full of girls and drink and jazz and books and decent
houses and decent jobs and being your own boss'.

Amis enjoyed at least the first four items on this
list when he returned to Oxford to complete his degree
course. Larkin, who was medically exempted from
military service, had left and become an academic
librarian, first in Belfast and then in Leicester. The two
men would never again live in the same place, but this
had the effect of provoking a rich correspondence
between them, and a visit by Amis to Leicester University which he claimed gave him the idea for *Lucky Jim*.
In Oxford he met an attractive young art student called
Hilary Bardwell and reported to Larkin his successful
campaign to get her to 'yield', and its sequel. In late
1947, after he had obtained a first-class degree and
commenced a B.Litt. course, Hilary became pregnant.

Amis arranged for her to have an abortion – a criminal, sordid, and expensive business in those days – but cancelled it at the last moment out of a creditable concern for Hilly's health, and they married. Amis retold the story in a late novel, *You Can't Do Both* (1994). Their son was born in August 1948, and named Philip, after Larkin. They were poor, but on the whole happy, Amis's main complaint about marriage being the new relatives he acquired, especially his father-in-law whom he described to Larkin as 'an extraordinary old man like a music-loving lavatory attendant', and vowed to pillory in a book one day. Mr Bardwell was the model for Professor Welch in *Lucky Jim*, but he failed, or perhaps refused, to recognise himself in the character.

Lucky Jim, however, was still in the future. At this time Amis was working on a novel called 'The Legacy'. Interestingly the main character was called 'Kingsley Amis' (a postmodernist trick which Amis never employed again, though his son Martin would use it in *Money*) and is described by Leader as Amis's 'first hero as shit'. Amis attributed his failure to find a publisher for the novel to its experimental character, and this may have motivated him to adopt a more reader-friendly style in his next fictional project. The B.Litt. course entailed writing a substantial dissertation, and the topic Amis proposed, later drastically reduced in scope, was significant: a study of the 'Decline of the Audience for Poetry 1850 to the Present Day', aiming to show that when poets neglected a large public readership their poetry suffered in quality. A view of writing as communication, rather than self-expression or the exploration of form, would become a fundamental principle of the Movement.

In 1949, without having finished his thesis, but with a second child (Martin) on the way, Amis applied for teaching posts at several universities and finally obtained one at University College Swansea, part of the federal University of Wales. Its English Department was not academically distinguished: no member of staff had published anything in the previous year, and with one exception none of them would ever publish a book. In this company Amis, with some published poetry and literary journalism to his name, was almost a star, and he kept his job even after his B.Litt. thesis was rejected by the two examiners, one of whom was Lord David Cecil. Amis was popular with students, though not always with his senior academic colleagues. It was in Swansea that he became a dedicated philanderer, and Hilly herself had occasional flings and one serious affair. It is likely that her third child, Sally, born in 1954, was not Amis's, though he never said or showed that this was the case. They became the centre of a raffish social scene, generous and permissive party hosts, especially after the sensational success of *Lucky Jim* in 1954.

That novel went through several drafts over several years, guided by extensive comments from Philip Larkin, especially when Amis was rewriting the penultimate version, entitled 'Dixon and Christine', which was submitted to and rejected by the publisher Michael Joseph. Leader gives a detailed and fascinating account of this revision process, during which Amis constantly consulted Larkin, who assisted him to a remarkable extent, suggesting significant changes in emphasis and structure which Amis invariably adopted. 'The help Larkin gave Amis with *Lucky Jim* was crucial to its success, as Amis

fulsomely acknowledged, both in public and private,' says
Leader. Larkin could not, however, conceal from other
friends some jealousy of the literary fame *Lucky Jim* and
its successors brought to Amis, and developed a grievance
against him on this score. Leader observes: 'In later years
Larkin would sometimes grumble about not being prop-
erly credited for the amount of help he gave Amis with
Lucky Jim. He once told Maeve Brennan . . . that Amis
had "stolen" *Lucky Jim* from him. He cannot, though . . .
have meant this seriously.' The success of the novel did,
however, significantly affect their friendship, as did Amis's
reports of his ever-accumulating sexual conquests, which
Larkin received with a mixture of astonishment, disapproval and envy that he put into a poem, 'Letter to a
Friend About Girls', which he wrote in 1959 and revised
at intervals up till 1970. He was never completely happy
with it, and by his own wish it was not published in his
lifetime. It begins:

> After comparing lives with you for years
> I see how I've been losing: all the while
> I've met a different gauge of girl from yours.
> Grant that, and all the rest makes sense as well.

And it ends:

> It's strange we never meet each other's sort:
> There should be equal chances, I'd've thought.
> Must finish now. One day perhaps I'll know
> What makes you be so lucky in your ratio.

One of those 'more things', could it be? *Horatio.*

The last line, which identifies the poem as a letter from Horatio to Hamlet, alluding to a famous speech in Shakespeare's play ('There are more things in heaven and earth, Horatio . . .') seems an obvious afterthought designed to disguise its biographical and autobiographical sources.*

Amis's philandering, and Hilly's less promiscuous infidelities, seem to have reached a kind of peak during the latter part of a year spent in America at Princeton University in 1958–9, where he gave the Gauss Seminars at the invitation of R.P. Blackmur (choosing science fiction as his topic, on the shrewd assumption that his audience would not know much about it) and taught

* Two items in Anthony Thwaite's edition of *Selected Letters* (1992) throw interesting light on this poem. In a letter to Thwaite in March 1970, Larkin revealed that in an earlier draft the line ended: 'could it be, Horatio?' making the poem a letter from Hamlet to Horatio, 'which may make better or worse sense, according to whether you think Horatio was a nicer chap than Hamlet or not'. He also explained what the poem 'was *meant* to do . . . to postulate a situation where, in the eyes of the author, his friend got all the straightforward easy girls and he got all the neurotic difficult ones, leaving the reader to see that in fact the girls were all the same, and simply responded to the way they were treated. In other words the difference was in the friends and not in the girls.' There were in fact significant differences between the women that Larkin and Amis were respectively involved with, but undoubtedly it was their own different characters and temperaments that determined the patterns of their sexual lives. In January 1978 Larkin reread the poem and commented in a letter to Thwaite: 'My reaction was that in the first place it wasn't at all funny: very sad and true; in the second, that the "joke" was either too obvious or too subtle to be seen.' For these and other reasons he concluded: 'we'll have to leave it to the posthumous volume.' That was Anthony Thwaite's edition of the *Collected Poems* (1988).

creative writing. Leader describes it as 'the wildest year
of their marriage'. Amis and Hilly had simultaneous
affairs with their neighbours the McAndrews, and
according to one observer, Betty Fussell, they 'inspired a
whole year of husband-and-wife-swapping' at Princeton,
though Kingsley was the main instigator, propositioning
every attractive woman he met regardless of her marital
status. 'It was compulsive,' commented another
Princeton friend. Amis's own explanation, or excuse,
was that for him sex was a way of exorcising the fear
of death, and this theme can be discerned in his fourth
novel, *Take a Girl Like You* (1960), whose hero muses
in characteristic Amis style:

> All that type of stuff, dying and so on, was a
> long way off, not such a long way off as it had
> once been, admitted, and no doubt the time
> when it wouldn't be such a long way off as all
> that wasn't such a long way off as all that, but
> still. Still what?

Take a Girl Like You describes the long campaign of the
cynical and selfish Patrick Standish to overcome the old-
fashioned moral principles of the heroine, Jenny Bunn,
and take her virginity. It was a carefully crafted novel
of acute social observation, a kind of elegy for an era of
sexual decorum and restraint that would soon be super-
seded by the permissive society, and that Amis had already
left far behind in private life.

Swansea must have seemed even more of an
academic backwater on their return from Princeton,
and Amis seriously considered settling in America, but

the offer of a fellowship at Peterhouse College, Cambridge kept him in England. He was, however, never really comfortable in this post. It was a college appointment in which the University's English Faculty had no say, and Amis was cold-shouldered by some of the latter's members. F.R. Leavis famously remarked that Peterhouse had hired 'a pornographer' (revealing complete ignorance of Amis's novels or pornography, or both, for Amis's fictional treatment of sexual intercourse is notably reticent). Peterhouse was hospitable but not much interested in literature as a subject. (It was symptomatic that an economic historian among the Fellows couldn't see what was funny about the title of Dixon's article in *Lucky Jim*.) Also Amis's tutoring duties, which he carried out conscientiously, were quite taxing. In 1962 he met Robert Graves, the visiting Professor of Poetry at Oxford, whose work he had always admired, and this led to a visit to Graves's home in Deya, Majorca, that summer, which was so enjoyable that Amis decided to resign his fellowship in 1963 and spend a year with his family on the island. It was a surprising decision for a writer who had famously attacked the literary cult of 'abroad', in *I Like It Here*, and Leader plausibly speculates that Amis had reached some kind of dead end in his life from which he was desperate to escape, like the anti-hero of the novel on which he was then working, *One Fat Englishman*. I shall return to this interesting novel.

The planned year with the family in Majorca did not happen. At this juncture Amis met the novelist Elizabeth

Jane Howard, appropriately and fatefully at a literary
festival seminar on Sex in Literature. Jane, as she was
known familiarly, was posh, talented, and beautiful, in
her second unhappy marriage. They began a passionate
affair, perhaps his first real *love* affair, which eventually
brought about the end of both marriages. Hilly went
to Majorca with the children and Amis moved in with
Jane in London. In due course they occupied a rather
grand house on the northern outskirts of London called
Lemmons and looked after Amis's two boys, Philip and
Martin, while Hilly had custody of Sally. For a while
everything went swimmingly. Amis continued to turn
out novels every two years or so, some of them clever
exercises in genre fiction, like *The Green Man* (1969) a
ghost story, *The Riverside Villas Murder* (1973) a period
whodunit, and *The Alteration* (1976) an alternative-world
tale. Over the same period Amis renounced his early
socialist leanings and – partly under the influence of his
old friend the historian Robert Conquest (whose First
Law was 'everybody is reactionary on subjects they
know about') and partly out of a mischievous delight
in bucking the cultural trend – became a notorious
media pundit of right-wing views, supporting the American war in Vietnam and opposing the expansion of
university education with the slogan, 'More will mean
Worse'. Meanwhile Jane bore the brunt of maintaining
a country house lifestyle without adequate funds, and
got very little writing done herself. Fault lines developed
in the marriage. Amis was drinking heavily, with
damaging effects on his libido which sex therapy failed
to cure – an experience he explored with astonishing
candour in *Jake's Thing* (1978). Reading this book Jane

came to the conclusion that he not only didn't love her any more, but didn't much like her, and after a couple more years of increasingly acrimonious relations, she left him.

Amis's physical health and morale declined steeply. Only the lifelong discipline of writing every morning between breakfast and the first drink at noon kept him going. Even so, it took him four years instead of his usual two to produce a new novel, and *Stanley and the Women* (1984) proved so bitterly (and craftily) misogynist that some women publishers in America did their best to suppress the book. To excessive drinking he added excessive eating, and grew obese. He had a fall and broke his leg. He desperately needed someone to look after him, and providentially Hilly, now married to an impecunious member of the House of Lords, Alastair Kilmarnock, was willing to take on the job in return for living rent-free with her husband in Amis's house. Martin attributes to Hilly's return his father's recovery from the slough of despond into which Jane's departure had pitched him, evidenced by the more balanced (though still quite dark) treatment of sexuality and gender in *The Old Devils* (1986), and *Difficulties with Girls* (1988).

With the award of the Booker Prize for the first of these books and a knighthood in 1990, Sir Kingsley Amis was set up to become a grand old man of English letters, but his last years were not serene. He developed a 'late style' which was almost as syntactically intricate as Henry James's, but without the latter's compensatory poetic eloquence or the wit of his own earlier novels, and previously loyal readers began to desert him. Drink continued to damage his body and could not exorcise his inner demons. His final illness was a distressing combination of physical collapse and mental derangement. Martin recalled that he and Philip, keeping watch beside the hospital bed of their apparently comatose father, were startled to hear him suddenly say, 'I am in hell.' Fundamentalist Christian moralists would no doubt see his unhappy end as divine punishment of an impenitent sinner, but his case was more complex and more interesting than that.

Not long before his death in October 1995 I spoke at a provincial literary festival a day or two after Kingsley Amis, and read by chance an interview with him in the local newspaper in which he shocked the young woman journalist by his aggressive, alcohol-fuelled responses to her innocent questions, snarling at one point: 'There is no God and life is absurd.' At his memorial service, Martin recalled his father's encounter with the Russian poet Yevgeny Yevtushenko, who said, 'You atheist?' and Kingsley replied, 'Well, yes, but it's more that I hate him.' In a 1987 essay entitled 'Godforsaken' he declared that 'human beings without faith are the poorer for it in every part of their lives'. Putting these disparate sentiments together we might deduce that Amis saw the world as a very dark place which was intolerable without transcendence, in the possibility of which he could not believe. The novel in which he explored most frankly the personal implications of this metaphysical double-bind was *One Fat Englishman*.

In 1963, when I was a young university lecturer, I published an essay in the *Critical Quarterly* entitled

'The Modern, the Contemporary, and the Importance of Being Amis', one of the earliest articles about the work of Kingsley Amis to appear in an academic journal, in which I discussed his four novels, from *Lucky Jim* to *Take a Girl Like You*. *One Fat Englishman* was published in the same year, too late to be included, but when I reprinted my essay in a book called *Language of Fiction*, in 1966, I did not extend it to discuss that novel. The reason for this silence was that I was uncertain what to make of *One Fat Englishman*, and it certainly didn't fit the general drift of my argument. I hadn't really enjoyed reading it, and enjoyment was very much at the heart of my interest in Amis's earlier fiction. Those books, I wrote, 'speak to me in an idiom, a tone of voice, to which I respond with immediate understanding and pleasure'. Their heroes were quick to identify and satirically subvert any hint of pretension, affectation, snobbery, vanity, and hypocrisy in public and private life. What they stood for is most simply described as 'decency', and when they didn't live up to their own code they felt appropriate remorse. The least ethical of these heroes, Patrick Standish in *Take a Girl Like You*, is partly redeemed by his attraction to the transparently decent heroine, Jenny Bunn, whose point of view complements and balances his.

Roger Micheldene, the corpulent British publisher whose adventures on a brief business trip to America are chronicled in *One Fat Englishman*, is a very different character. He is rude, arrogant, snobbish, lecherous, treacherous, greedy and totally selfish. While trying to revive an affair with Helene, the wife of a Danish philologist, he grabs every opportunity to copulate with other available women. His thoughts, and often his speech, are crammed with offensive observations about Jews, Negroes, women, homosexuals and Americans in general. He eats like a pig and drinks like a fish. He is quite conscious of these traits and habits, and perversely proud of them: 'Of the seven deadly sins, Roger considered himself qualified in gluttony, sloth and lust, but distinguished in anger.'

The story punishes Roger for his sins by submitting him to a series of farcical humiliations, and eventually he is sent home with his tail between his legs. But he is the hero, or anti-hero, of the novel, whose consciousness totally dominates it and with whom the authorial voice is rhetorically in collusion. That is to say, his obnoxious opinions and reactions are articulated through the same distinctive stylistic devices that were associated with the earlier and more amiable Amis heroes. The reader may guiltily catch himself sniggering at lines like: 'At this evasion a part of Roger . . . wanted to step forward and give Helene a medium-weight slap across the chops' or 'a girl of Oriental appearance who would have been quite acceptable if she had had eye sockets as well as eyes'. In 1963, knowing little about Kingsley Amis except through his writings, I was puzzled to know why he had taken such pains to create this vividly unpleasant character. In my memory, most other fans of his work were equally baffled and disappointed. But in the light of Amis's subsequent literary development, and all the biographical information that has emerged since his death, *One Fat Englishman* seems a much more comprehensible and interesting novel – also funnier, in its black way – than

I remembered on first reading it. It now seems obvious that Roger Micheldene was in several respects a devastating and prophetic self-portrait.

The character's promiscuous womanising and inordinate drinking, as we now know, had autobiographical sources. On his return to England from Princeton Amis boasted in a letter to Larkin: 'I was boozing and fucking harder than at any time . . . On the second count I was at it practically full-time . . . you have to take what you can get when you can get it, you sam.' (This substitution of 'sam' for 'see' was part of the private language in which they communicated.) He was writing *One Fat Englishman* when he met Elizabeth Jane Howard in 1962. Hilly soon discovered the affair, and accompanied Kingsley on a pre-arranged trip to Italy and Yugoslavia in an unhappy mood. When he fell asleep on the beach one day she wrote on his exposed back in lipstick: 'I FAT ENGLISHMAN – I FUCK ANYTHING'. (A photograph of this vengeful *graffito* was reproduced in Eric Jacobs's biography.) Jane read the novel in manuscript as he was finishing it in the summer of 1963, and recalled later: 'The awfulness of Roger Micheldene really shocked me. Apart from it being funny, it was so horrible.' They were enjoying a working holiday in Spain at the time, and she evidently did not suspect that Amis was projecting an extreme version of the man he might turn into.

Although, as the 1962 photo shows, Kingsley was not really fat at that time, he became so later, and as gluttonous as Roger Micheldene. But whereas for Roger this is an appetite that competes for priority with the sexual (at one point, having picked up a girl at a

bring-your-own-picnic, he worries about 'the problem
of retaining contact with Suzanne without giving her
anything to eat'), for Kingsley, according to Martin in
Experience, it displaced sex after his marriage to Jane
ended: 'getting fat was more like a project, grimly
inaugurated on the day Jane left him in the winter of
1980 . . . a complex symptom, repressive, self-isolating.
It cancelled him out sexually.' It is clear from the
biographical record that Jane left Amis for much the
same reasons as Helene finally rejects Roger (not before
time, the reader may think) in *One Fat Englishman*.

The parallels are ideological as well as personal. *One
Fat Englishman* was written on the cusp of Amis's movement from left to right, written almost exactly halfway
between the Fabian pamphlet of 1957 in which he
declared his allegiance to the Labour Party, and the 1967
essay 'Why Lucky Jim Turned Right' which announced
his conversion to conservatism. Many of his prejudices
were anticipated by Roger Micheldene, but in the novel
they have an ambivalent import. It is as if Kingsley Amis,
conscious in the early 1960s of the way his values and
opinions were changing, and himself half-appalled by the
process, projected them into a fictional character he could
simultaneously identify with and invite the reader to
condemn. In a curious and interesting way Roger is
similarly divided about himself. 'Why are you so awful?'
Helene asks him at a moment of post-coital candour.
'Yes, I used to ask myself that quite a lot,' he replies.
'Not so much of late however.' She finds this honesty
disarming, which is exactly the effect he calculated – but
it is not *just* calculation.

Roger is really full of self-hatred – it is the source

of the vitriolic anger he directs at almost everything and everybody in the world around him – and it is hard to disagree with the judgement of the American Catholic priest, Father Colgate, absurd figure though he is: 'You are in acute spiritual pain.' That Roger is a Roman Catholic of an idiosyncratic kind, who addresses God familiarly in prayer between breaking as many command-ments as possible, is one of the ways in which Amis distanced himself from his anti-hero – but not so far as it might seem. Roger's rejection of Father Colgate's counsel is a theological harangue that anticipates Amis's remark to Yevtushenko in 1962 about hating God: 'Has it never occurred to you that we're bound to God by ties of fear and anger and resentment as well as love? And do you know what despair is like?'

We take leave of Roger weeping tears he is unable to explain as his ship slides out of New York harbour, and resolving to lift his mood by surveying the shipboard totty. 'Something in him was less than enthusiastic about this course of action but he resolved to ignore it. Better a bastard than a bloody fool, he told it.' Father Colgate would call that maxim 'Obstinacy in Sin', while Jim Dixon would have turned it the other way round. *One Fat Englishman* is certainly a much less comfortable read than *Lucky Jim*, but no longer seems as inferior to it as I once thought. To write a novel entirely from the point of view of a totally unsympathetic character is a very daring and difficult undertaking, but Amis manages to bring it off by making Roger's transgressive awfulness the engine of anarchic comedy. The reader's inclination to recoil in disgust is invariably checked by an irresistible impulse to laugh, though the laughter is always uneasy.

In an obituary of him I said that Kingsley Amis's vision was in its way as bleak as Samuel Beckett's, but cushioned and concealed by the conventions of the well-made novel. I should have inserted a rider, 'from *One Fat Englishman* onwards'. With that qualification I stick to the comparison, much as it would have surprised and annoyed Kingsley Amis.

Postscript

New light was thrown on the relationship between Kingsley Amis and Philip Larkin by the latter's remarkable correspondence with Monica Jones over some forty years, discovered after her death and not published until 2010 (*Letters to Monica*, ed. Anthony Thwaite). When Larkin received the final revised typescript of *Lucky Jim*, the response he reported to her was generous and enthusiastic:

> I must say that *Lucky Jim* is now, to my mind, one of the funniest books I've ever read, at least I *think* so. Only a printed copy can settle the question finally. But I don't think anything can stop it being a howling success; it seems to me so entirely original that my own suggestions really pass unnoticed, as they were for the most part concerned with structure and plot. I don't myself think anyone has been funny in this way before, and that even if he never writes anything else it will remain as a landmark.

After *Lucky Jim* was the howling success he predicted, the tone of Larkin's references to Amis changed noticeably. On 15 February 1955 he tells Monica:

> Kingsley never writes. I shouldn't be surprised if he were fed up with me, in a shoulder-shrugging sort of way: I am of him, except as you say 'the dog is so very comical.' I was interested to hear that the book [Amis's second novel, *That Uncertain Feeling*, just completed] had gone to Gollancz – oh please God, make them return it, with a suggestion he 'rewrites certain passages'! Nothing would please me more. And I refuse to believe he can write a book on his own – at least a good one. Still, we'll see. In a sense he has behaved more consistently than I have: I sought his company because it gave me such a wonderful sense of relief – I've always wanted this 'fourth form friend' with whom I can pretend that things are *not* as they are – and pretended I was like him. Now I don't feel like pretending any longer, and I suppose it looks like 'turning against him', although it's not really . . . Probably he has been mistaken, to himself, about me.

When Larkin reads a favourable review of *That Uncertain Feeling* in the *New Statesman* just before obtaining a copy, he writes to Monica, on 19 August 1955: 'What the *NS&N* terms a brilliantly funny opening scene in a public library is, I am prepared to swear, taken from one of my Wellington letters. *I remember writing it:* "a sample

encounter with a borrower." . . . It irritates me power-
fully to see this stuff, small though it may be, used for
his credit & advantage.' A couple of days later, having
read the novel, he admits, 'I was piling it on in the first
scene, really, though there are spills & spars of a dialogue
of mine in it. I contribute about 4 other gags in the
course of the book, but they've mostly been adapted.'
Some years later (11 October 1960) he reports congratu-
lating Robert Conquest 'on replacing me as chief unpaid
unacknowledged gagman to Amis Inc.'.

One can understand Larkin's sore feelings about
the irony of his situation. There is always an element
of rivalry in a friendship between artists in the same
field, and Larkin found he had helped Amis to achieve
a level of success and income neither of them had
anticipated, and which was in painful contrast to the
muted reception and sales of his own two published
novels, *Jill* and *A Girl in Winter*. It was not coincidental
that he never completed the third novel he had started
before *Lucky Jim* was published. Basic differences of
character and attitude between the two men which
had previously been latent became overt as time went
on, and relations cooled to the extent that contact
ceased for some years in the 1960s, after which they
were undemonstratively reconciled and resumed their
correspondence, though not with the spontaneity and
frequency of old.

In 2012 Richard Bradford, who had previously
published biographies of both Amis (in 2001) and Larkin
(in 2009), retraced the history of their relationship in
*The Odd Couple: The Curious Friendship between Kingsley
Amis and Philip Larkin*, drawing on *Letters to Monica* and

unpublished letters by Amis, and adding a good deal of tendentious speculation of his own. But he is probably correct in suggesting that Larkin's increasing eminence as a poet enabled him to overcome his envy of Amis's success.

A TRICKY UNDERTAKING: THE BIOGRAPHY OF MURIEL SPARK

M URIEL SPARK PUBLISHED twenty-two novels in
her lifetime, despite beginning relatively late at
the age of thirty-nine, and at least half of them are classics by the only criterion that really matters – they invite
and reward repeated rereading. She was arguably the most
innovative British novelist writing in the second half of
the twentieth century, extending the possibilities of fiction
for other writers as well as for herself. Arriving on the
English literary scene in the late 1950s, she challenged
the aesthetic principles not only of the neo-realist novel
of that decade, but also of the modernist novel from
Henry James to Virginia Woolf, demonstrating a different
style of story-telling we would learn to call postmodernist.
She took the convention of the omniscient author familiar
in classic nineteenth-century novels and applied it in a
new, speeded-up, throwaway style to artfully contrived
plots of a kind rare in twentieth-century literary fiction.
Instead of hiding behind a character-narrator or culti-
vating a modernist 'impersonality', Spark's authorial voice
was up front, briskly summarising the characters and their
actions, and shifting the temporal focus of the story – not
with the deliberation of Joseph Conrad or Ford Madox
Ford, but at dizzying speed, from present to past to future

and back again, sometimes in a single paragraph. Solemn
subjects, like guilt, religious faith and death, were dealt
with in a bright and sparkling epigrammatic style. The
supernatural, in the form of angels and devils, and the
uncanny, like the untraceable telephone calls which
remind the characters in *Memento Mori* that they must
die, are apt to intrude disconcertingly into the modern
secular world. She was, I believe, a liberating influence
on a fertile generation of English women novelists that
included Beryl Bainbridge, Fay Weldon, Alice Thomas
Ellis and (in some of her work) Hilary Mantel. She herself
had no obvious precursors, except perhaps Ivy Compton-
Burnett. It is interesting to learn from Martin Stannard's
biography★ that Spark was in her formative years an
enthusiastic reader of Compton-Burnett, whose work
however has a much narrower range of themes and effects
than her own.

A truly original writer is a very rare bird, whose appearance is apt to disconcert other birds and bird-watchers.
I was beginning my own career as a novelist and critic
when Muriel Spark began publishing her fiction: in the
former capacity I was under the influence of the neo-
realism of the 1950s and as a critic I revered the great
modernists like Henry James, Conrad and Joyce. I was
also interested in something called the Catholic Novel
and had recently completed a thesis on the subject with
concluding chapters on Evelyn Waugh and Graham
Greene. Muriel Spark didn't fit into any of these

★ *Muriel Spark: the Biography* (2009).

categories, and although she was a convert to the Roman Catholic faith, and publicly admired by Greene and Waugh, her take on it was very different from theirs. Reviewing *The Prime of Miss Jean Brodie* in 1961, I declared myself 'beguiled . . . but not really stirred or involved or enlightened'. It was some time before I recognised it as a masterpiece and tried to make amends with an extended appreciation of the novel in my book *The Novelist at the Crossroads* (1971).

There were, however, enough readers in the 1960s impressed by the wit, sharp observation and refreshing novelty of Spark's narrative style to make her into a literary star quite quickly, especially in America. *The New Yorker* dedicated nearly a whole issue of the magazine to a slightly shortened version of *The Prime of Miss Jean Brodie*, only the second time it had conferred such an honour. Nevertheless (a key word in Spark's own vocabulary, one she heard often in childhood from the lips of scrupulous Scottish matrons) there was nearly always a significant mutter of dissent and dissatisfaction audible in the general buzz of approbation that greeted each new work, and it grew in volume as she became more and more uncompromisingly experimental in form and content. Reviewing *The Only Problem* in 1984, Frank Kermode described her as 'our best novelist' but added: 'Although she is admired and giggled at, I doubt if this estimate is widely shared. This may be because virtuosos, especially cold ones, aren't thought serious enough. Another reason is that although we have a special niche for certain religious novels, Mrs Spark's kind of religion seems bafflingly idiosyncratic.' Martin Stannard quotes this shrewd observation and his meticulous biography helps us to fill out and understand its implications.

The history of this work is itself of interest. In 1992 Muriel Spark wrote an approving review of the second volume of Stannard's biography of Evelyn Waugh and when he thanked her for it, she replied that she hoped she would be fortunate enough to find as sympathetic a biographer one day. Stannard tentatively offered his own services, and she invited him to visit her in Tuscany to discuss this 'interesting idea'. Soon he was invited to write an authorised biography. No professional (or professorial) biographer could have resisted the opportunity, and he seized it, while wondering why a writer known for fiercely guarding her privacy should allow a total stranger to investigate her life without conditions. He was guaranteed independence, made free of a huge archive of her papers, and exhorted to 'write about me as though I were dead'. Spark had just finished writing *Curriculum Vitae*, a memoir of her early life up to the publication of her first novel, and Stannard surmised that she resented the expenditure of time and energy required by this task, and decided to let someone else continue it while she got on with her creative work.

Writing a biography of a living person is always a tricky undertaking, and Muriel Spark was no exception. She had been prompted to write *Curriculum Vitae* to correct what she regarded as misrepresentations of herself in an unauthorised biography by Derek Stanford, her lover and literary collaborator in the years before she became famous, and, as Stannard would soon discover, she was notorious for making imperious demands of her publishers, and frequently threatening to sue others for publishing false reports about her. The pile of documents made accessible to Stannard proved to contain nothing that was personally revealing, and indeed seemed more like a wall designed to conceal her private life. It was unlikely that such a volatile and controlling personality would maintain the promised hands-off stance towards her biography, and so it proved. Although Stannard has maintained a discreet silence on the subject, it is well known that when Spark read his finished manuscript she declared that it was 'unfair' to her, and withheld permission to publish it, a ban that was maintained for some time by her literary executor after her death in 2006. How the dispute was resolved we do not know, but this long-delayed book displays no trace of the frustration its author endured: its account of Muriel Spark impresses one as both sympathetic and accurate.

Muriel Spark was born in Edinburgh in February 1918, the final year of the most terrible war the world had ever known, a circumstance she exploited in a brilliant magic-realist story 'The First Year of My Life', in which the preternaturally perceptive infant narrator comments caustically but silently on the folly and evil of the adult world in which she finds herself. Muriel's father Bernard 'Barney' Camberg was a Jew, her mother Sarah ('Cissy') was according to her daughter half-Jewish, with a Christian mother, though the ambiguity of this lineage was to prove a source of much trouble in Muriel's later years. There is, however, no reason to doubt her assertion that family life was not noticeably Jewish in matters of diet and ritual observances, that they rarely attended synagogue, and that its general ethos was liberal and secular. Socially they were at the top end of the working class, Barney being a skilled factory worker, and Cissy the offspring of small shopkeepers in Watford in the south of England. She seems to have been an amiable but rather lazy woman who, Stannard startlingly reveals, consumed a bottle of Madeira every day. That fact shows they were not poor, but their accommodation was limited: when Cissie's widowed mother came to live with them Muriel had to give up her bedroom and slept for five years on a sofa in the kitchen. It is hard to imagine a modern teenager putting up with this for five days, but Spark claimed that she suffered no sense of deprivation. She found her grandmother an object of intense interest and helped uncomplainingly to care for her after she suffered a stroke and became bedridden and demented – experience which later bore fruit in *Memento Mori*.

Neither of Muriel's parents, Stannard observes, 'had the faintest interest in literature' and nor did her elder brother, Philip, who became an engineer. Her own interest was stimulated and fed primarily through education at the James Gillespie School which she attended from the age of five to seventeen. It was there that she fell into the hands of a teacher called Miss Kay, or, as she later wrote, 'it might be said that she fell into my hands' for Miss Kay was the model for Miss Brodie, whose 'dazzling non-sequiturs' she would later adapt as a compositional device. She also developed a fruitful friendship with a fellow pupil, Frances Niven, with whom she shared a passionate interest in reading and writing poetry, and made her debut in print at the age of twelve with five poems in an anthology called *The*

Door of Youth. The following year, 1932, she entered a competition open to all Edinburgh schools for a poem on Sir Walter Scott, the centenary of whose death was then being celebrated, and won first prize.

It wasn't just her family's limited means that prevented this obviously gifted girl from proceeding to university, for there were scholarships that might have been found for the purpose: Muriel herself had no great urge to do so. She sensed, probably correctly, that the academic study of literature would prevent her from exploring it in her own idiosyncratic way, and was anxious to make herself employable in the economically depressed 1930s. So she enrolled in business-oriented college courses in shorthand typing and précis-writing which stood her in good stead in the years to come, bringing her a variety of jobs that were not always rewarding in themselves but provided invaluable material for fiction (and no doubt helped to form her lucid, economical prose style). Three more years of formal education might have saved her from a disastrous marriage, but even that brought her experience she was able to turn to positive account in fiction. As the narrator of *Loitering with Intent*, Fleur Talbot, says: 'everything happens to an artist; time is always redeemed, nothing is lost and wonders never cease.'

The sexual liaisons and intrigues among the teachers and pupils which drive the plot of *The Prime of Miss Jean Brodie*, were, as Spark admitted, a fictional addition to the reality of her schooldays. Edinburgh in the 1930s was an intensely puritanical society, and premarital sex was simply not an option for a respectable young woman. 'I never slept with anyone before I got married, because

no-one anyway ever asked me,' she told Stannard. 'You
didn't. There wouldn't have been anywhere to go. I
wasn't in that way of life.' But she had boyfriends, and
to the surprise of her friends and the dismay of her father
she accepted at the age of nineteen a proposal of marriage
from one of them, Sydney Oswald Spark, who was
thirteen years older than herself and whom none of them
liked or trusted. Why? He had an MA in Mathematics
from Edinburgh University which may have impressed
her, and she evidently enjoyed being the object of his
infatuation, but if sex was a motive it was probably
driven more by curiosity than desire on her part. (She
told an interviewer in 1974 that she had rushed into
marriage because it was then 'the only way to get sex'.)
That 'Ossie' as she called him (or later, 'S.O.S.') was a
non-practising Jew perhaps made him seem a compatible
spouse, given her own tenuous sense of Jewish identity;
and he offered her an opportunity to see something of
the great world, for he intended to go to Southern
Rhodesia (now Zimbabwe) on a three-year teaching
contract. He did not tell her, however, that he had been
unable to hold down a teaching job in Scotland and had
been seeing a psychiatrist.

Ossie preceded Muriel to Africa, and they were
married there in September 1937. The wedding night
was inauspicious – 'An awful mess. Awful. Such a botch-
up,' she commented years later – but she was soon pregnant, and soon aware too of her husband's unstable
character. She responded to the beauty of the African
landscape, and the friendliness of the natives, but the
arrogance and philistinism of white colonial society
oppressed her, and combined with the increasingly

threatening behaviour of her husband to precipitate a
depression after her son Robin was born. Before long
the Sparks were effectively separated. (Coincidentally
another future novelist of distinction, Doris Lessing, was
going through similar experience a few hundred miles
away, but they were unknown to each other.) By the
time the Second World War broke out Muriel was determined to return to the UK where she hoped to arrange
for a divorce with custody of her child, and, after leaving
Robin in the care of a Catholic convent school and
moving to South Africa, she eventually arrived in a war-
worn London in March 1944 and joyfully embraced its
dangers and austerities (see *The Girls of Slender Means*).
Her familiarity with the novels of Ivy Compton-Burnett
sufficiently impressed an interviewer at the Foreign Office
to land her a fascinating job in Sefton Delmer's 'Black
Propaganda' department, confusing the German population with radio broadcasts that cunningly mixed truth
with invention (see *The Hothouse by the East River*).

When the war ended she sent for Robin, but to her
surprise and dismay he arrived accompanied by Ossie,
who was not disposed to be co-operative about a divorce.
He had resumed Jewish orthodoxy and was inculcating
this in Robin to make the child bond with him rather
than Muriel, while Robin, one may surmise, already had
reason to feel that his mother had deserted him in infancy.
Her solution to this imbroglio was to leave Robin in
Edinburgh in the care of her mother, and go to London
to start a literary career. It was, judged by normal maternal
standards, a selfish decision, but it was selfishness for art's
sake. She was convinced that she was born to be a writer
and throughout her life allowed nothing to stand in the

way of that vocation. For a long time she pursued it as a poet, supporting herself in a variety of low-paid jobs associated with publishing and editing, and by producing literary biographies and anthologies, mostly in collaboration with Derek Stanford whom she met through the Poetry Society. This was then a haven for old-fashioned and mediocre versifiers, with some of whom she had flirtations and affairs, and with others feuds when she became the society's secretary and the editor of its magazine.

She was in some danger of languishing in this genteel end of Grub Street indefinitely, with no more than a sheaf of rejection slips to show for her poems, when in December 1950 she won a competition for a short story on a Christmas theme sponsored by the *Observer* newspaper which attracted nearly 7,000 entries. Her story, 'The Seraph and the Zambesi', described an angel gate-crashing a rather tawdry nativity play in Rhodesia in a manner both vivid and matter-of-fact, which Stannard plausibly suggests was the first example of magic realism in British writing. It seems to have been also the first piece of prose fiction Spark wrote for publication, and yet it instantly demonstrated that *this* − not verse − was the medium in which she could fulfil her artistic ambitions. 'The whole tone of the narrative', Stannard justly observes, 'is suddenly lighter than that of the poetry, rippling with crisp, implicit mockery.' She never was, and never would be, a great poet in verse, but her novels and novellas are essentially poetic in style and structure.

This success was her first taste of fame, but she did not consolidate it rapidly or easily, for reasons to do with her troubled state of body and soul at the time.

Stannard is particularly illuminating on this phase of her life, when she was moving towards Christian faith, first in the Anglican and finally in the Roman Catholic Church, conducting an on-off sexual relationship with the much less gifted Stanford, and trying to write her first novel, while keeping solvent, and her name in the public eye, with literary journalism. She wrote a review of T.S. Eliot's play *The Confidential Clerk* which astonished the author with its insight, and his praise encouraged her to begin a critical study of Eliot's work, but she was overdosing on Dexadrine in order to suppress appetite and work longer hours, which had the effect of making her temporarily deranged and convinced that Eliot's writing was full of coded threatening messages to herself. All these experiences entered into her first novel, including the struggle to write it. *The Comforters* is about a young woman recently converted to Roman Catholicism who is having a nervous breakdown which takes the form of hearing an authorial voice tapping out on a phantom typewriter a prejudicial description of her thoughts in the novelistic third person. We would learn to call this 'metafiction'.

The Comforters was greatly admired when it was published in 1957, especially by Evelyn Waugh, who was struck by its similarities to *The Ordeal of Gilbert Pinfold* which he was currently writing. Graham Greene, who had already been impressed by some unpublished stories he had been shown by Stanford, and was generously giving Spark financial help, added his praise. These were the two most distinguished living English novelists at the time, and both Catholic converts. Muriel Spark 'completed a grand triumvirate of Catholic-convert novelists', Stannard declares at the outset of his book, but the Catholicism expressed in her fiction is very different from Waugh's unquestioning orthodoxy or Greene's obsession with sin and salvation – much more playful, speculative, and unsympathetic to typical Catholic piety. The dogmatic certainties on which the 'Catholic Novel' was based were, however, soon to be called into question by the Second Vatican Council and the emergence of a much more pluralistic Church than the one she originally joined, so her increasingly idiosyncratic Catholicism caused less of a stir than it might otherwise have done. She openly criticised the papacy, for instance, did not attend mass regularly, and always avoided the sermon when she did. Her attraction to the Faith was basically metaphysical: she liked the idea of a transcendental order of truth against which to measure human vanity and folly, and was fascinated by the similarities and differences between the omniscience of God, the fictive omniscience of novelists, and the dangerous pretensions to omniscience of human beings like Miss Brodie. *Sub specie aeternitatis* human life was not tragic or pathetic, but comic or absurd. 'I think it's bad manners to inflict a lot of emotional involvement on the reader – much nicer to make them laugh and to keep it short,' she told an interviewer in her deceptively insouciant style. This is what Kermode meant by the 'cold' quality of her work. In real life it could be disconcerting: he recalls that she could not see why a party he planned to give in New York in her honour should be cancelled because President Kennedy had been assassinated the day before, since 'he was only dead because God wanted him'. She was not, however, indifferent to the problem of reconciling the evil and suffering in the world with the idea of God – indeed she considered it 'the only problem' in theology. But, drawing on her Jewish heritage, she approached it through the Old Testament rather than the New, especially the book of Job, where God himself in her view becomes an absurd character.

Stannard sums up the relation between Spark's metaphysics and her fictional innovations perceptively: 'there was human time and there was God's time. She played with these two spheres of reality: using ghost narrators, revealing endings to destroy conventional suspense, starting at the end or in the middle, fracturing the plausible surfaces of obsessive detail with sudden discontinuities.' This daring deconstruction of the traditional realistic novel (and the realistic *noir* thriller) was most extreme in a sequence of short, spare novellas she produced in the late 1960s and the 1970s such as *The Driver's Seat* (her personal favourite among her fictions) and *Not to Disturb.* In the former a woman pursues across Rome the man who must murder her; in the latter a butler presides over a crime of passion in a Swiss villa in a manner that is both God-like and Jeeves-like. Among other things they helped to make present-tense narration, hitherto rarely used by novelists, almost the default mode of contemporary fiction. The general public and some reviewers found these books baffling, and she had more commercial success later with novels like *Loitering with Intent* and *A Far Cry from Kensington* that drew on her early life to the same droll effect as the early novels.

After scraping through the dreaded test of the second novel with *Robinson* (1958) she produced, at the rate of one a year, a sequence of scintillating novels from *Memento Mori* to *The Girls of Slender Means*, while living in the unfashionable London suburb of Camberwell under the protection of a motherly landlady, and making occasional, not very enjoyable duty visits to her family in Edinburgh, who she felt exploited her increased prosperity. It was perhaps partly to put them at a distance that in the late 1960s she based herself for long periods in New York, occupying an office of her own at *The New Yorker*. Later she settled in Rome, where she lived for many years in some style, escorted by a series of ornamental but usually gay or bisexual men. Stannard surmises that 'she did not discover their sexuality until too late' but one feels that, although she enjoyed dressing up glamorously and exerting her spell over men, subconsciously she did not want to be possessed by them and chose her male companions accordingly. From 1968 onwards she became more and more dependent on her friendship with Penelope Jardine, an artist resident in Rome, who acquired a derelict priest's house and adjoining church in Tuscany and converted them into a home where Muriel eventually joined her, with Penelope, who was fifteen years younger, acting as her companion and secretary. Spark calmly denied they were lesbians, but Stannard says it was love that bound them together. Perhaps 'a Boston marriage' best describes their relationship. Muriel bought a series of automobiles in which she enjoyed being driven around Europe by Penelope, who had a fear of flying.

Spark's later life was marred by illness and painful disability partly caused by incompetent medical care, which she endured with remarkable fortitude. She was less tolerant of what she considered harassment by her son, Robin, who accused her of denying her Jewish lineage and impugning his own by claiming that she was only 'half-Jewish'. The issue turned on the exact nature of her maternal grandmother's marriage, and the evidence, according to Stannard, is capable of different interpretations. Sadly this dispute permanently alienated mother and son, and brought Muriel some unfavourable publicity in Britain's scandal-hungry press, which continued after her death in 2006 when it was revealed that she had cut Robin out of her will.

She was, it must be admitted, a difficult as well as fascinating woman to know personally or professionally. She was mercurial in temperament, restless and demanding, quick to take offence, chameleon-like in appearance, and capable of seeming to be two different women on successive days, as I discovered myself on the only occasions when I met her, one weekend in Rome in 1974, halfway through an Italian lecture tour for the British Council. The first was a supper given by the head of the council's Roman office, when I was seated next to her. She was plainly dressed in a navy blue trouser suit which gave her (at that time) slender frame a gamine appearance, and was deferential to my academic status, though apparently unaware that I also wrote novels. More than once in the conversation, however, she claimed to know things which she had previously denied knowing. She had read my essay about *The Prime of Miss Jean Brodie*, and appreciated it, and also mentioned with satisfaction Frank Kermode's praise for her work – the approbation of academic critics evidently meant a lot to her. She told me that she had just finished a novel called *The Abbess of Crewe* based on

Watergate, which she thought would be her best. (It was not.) The next evening I was invited to a large party at her apartment where she was transformed into a glamorous hostess, wearing a flowing robe and with a bouffant hair-do, moving among her guests with regal aloofness, and I had little opportunity to speak to her. Some acquaintances regarded her as a kind of white witch gifted with preternatural insight. Most found her eccentric and unpredictable, and some thought she was a little mad – an insinuation which, if she ever heard of it, would cause their excommunication from her friendship. Some of those character traits pervade her fiction, which is challenging rather than ingratiating. But as the heroine of *Loitering with Intent*, a portrait of the young Muriel Spark as aspiring writer, observes: 'I wasn't writing poetry and prose so that the reader would think me a nice person, but in order that my sets of words should convey ideas of truth and wonder.' That aim the mature Spark triumphantly achieved.

JOHN BOORMAN'S QUEST

I HAVE A PERSONAL reason to feel very grateful to the film director John Boorman. In 1981 I was making notes for a comic novel about academics and writers jetting about the world to attend international conferences. I could think of plenty of amusing episodes and situations and representative character-types, including several from an earlier novel, *Changing Places*, but for a long time I was held up by the lack of a narrative structure to contain them all. In my notebook I wrote, 'Could some myth serve, as in *Ulysses*? *E.g.*, the Grail legend.' I was thinking of how James Joyce modelled his account of one day in the lives of a number of modern Dubliners on the story of Homer's *Odyssey*. But I did nothing with the idea until, a little later, I happened to see Boorman's film *Excalibur*, and was swept away by its exuberant and imaginative retelling of the Arthurian story. It set me thinking about correspondences between the Grail legend as it appears in chivalric romance and a modern story of academics and novelists competing with each other for professional glory and getting involved in amorous entanglements in various exotic settings. I started writing *Small World*.

There are many pleasures to be derived from John Boorman's autobiography, *Adventures of a Suburban*

Boy (2003), but for me its most interesting revelation was that the legendary quest for the cup used by Jesus at the Last Supper, incorporated by Malory in the *Morte d'Arthur*, and reinterpreted in modern times by Jessie Weston, T.S. Eliot and John Cowper Powys, among others, has deep roots in Boorman's own life and psyche, and is the key to his cinematic *oeuvre*. He read *The Waste Land* and Powys's *A Glastonbury Romance* as a teenager, excited and enraptured by these texts, and they made an enduring impression. His own book's unassuming title encodes a heroic meaning: a quest for the cinematic Grail, the ultimate transcendent film, was the serial adventure that allowed Boorman to escape the spiritual wasteland of suburbia.

His first childhood home was a semi-detached house in Rosehill Avenue, Carshalton, on the outskirts of London – one of 4 million built between the wars. 'Four million of them! . . . Was there ever such a stealthy social revolution as the rise of this semi-detached suburbia?' he asks rhetorically. 'They all missed it, or got it wrong – the academics, the politicians, the upper classes. While they worried about socialism and fascism, the cuckoo had laid its egg in their nests and Margaret Thatcher would hatch out of it.' Ironically, when he came to re-create his childhood in the Oscar-nominated *Hope and Glory*, he was obliged to build a simulated Rosehill Avenue on an abandoned airfield, because those streets of inter-war semis have been irrecoverably 'improved' – festooned with TV aerials, satellite dishes, double-glazed porches and other accoutrements of post-war affluence.

The Boormans had been affluent once. His paternal

grandfather was a cheerfully eccentric inventor and businessman, sufficiently well-off to send his sons to public
school, who lost all his money shortly after the First
World War. John's father George came back from interesting military service in India to painfully reduced
circumstances, and was obliged to take a clerical job
which he hated. He and his friend Herbert were both
captivated by Ivy, the beautiful daughter of a Wimbledon
publican. George popped the question and won her
hand, but Ivy had always secretly preferred Herbert, and
as the joy slowly leaked out of her marriage in the
confines of Rosehill Avenue she turned increasingly to
Herbert for solace. Thus was the triangular relationship
of Arthur–Guinevere–Lancelot re-enacted in Metroland.
The young John sensed what was going on, and felt
guiltily complicit in the betrayal of his father, but George,
embittered by the boring routine of his life, did not
inspire great filial affection. Sometimes John disloyally
wished that Herbert had been his dad.

The outbreak of the Second World War offered a kind
of deliverance for all parties from this drab, repressed existence. 'How wonderful was the war! . . . it gave us the
essential thing we lacked: it gave us a myth, a myth nurtured
by the wireless, newspapers, the cinema, that allowed us
semi people to leap our garden gates, vault over our embar-
rassments into the arms of patriotism.' George couldn't wait
to join up, though he was forty, but ironically, like many
servicemen, found himself posted to safe barracks in the
country while the bombs were falling on Rosehill Avenue.
'We kids rampaged through the ruins, the semis opened
up like dolls' houses, the precious privacy shamefully
exposed. We took pride in our collection of shrapnel.'

The pleasure and wonder that young boys, untroubled by adult anxieties, could derive from the Blitz were vividly evoked in *Hope and Glory*, but its most memorable scene belongs to a later phase of the war. In the First World War Ivy and her sisters had fled the threat of German Zeppelins by retreating to the Thames-side village of Shepperton where their father had a bungalow as a weekend retreat and holiday home. Now, driven by some atavistic urge, she took her own children back to Shepperton (still undeveloped and unspoiled) for safety, and so began John Boorman's lifelong romance with rivers, of which the Thames was the archetype. He swam, and fished, boated and punted, and fell into a lock while the sluice was open, narrowly escaping drowning – the first of many brushes with death in his life.

He attended the local C. of E. school and sang in the parish choir, but when he failed the 11 plus his mother sent him to a private Roman Catholic grammar school run by the Salesian order, where he experienced the culture of corporal punishment sadly characteristic of Catholic education in those days. 'The young brothers and priests seemed pent up, over-wound, their only release the infliction of pain.' No attempt was made to convert him, but a devout chum with a shaky grasp of the relevant theology insisted on baptising him secretly in the school toilets, pulling the chain and catching the water in his hand before it was polluted by the toilet bowl. 'I became, in a manner of speaking, a closet Catholic.' Perhaps John Boorman did in fact acquire from this schooling a feeling for ritual and symbolism that is more Catholic than Protestant, and which left its mark on his films.

Towards the end of the war the school was destroyed by a 'doodlebug' (the V1 flying bomb) just as the academic year was due to begin, an episode with which Boorman ends *Hope and Glory*, in the scene where the blazered schoolboys deliriously celebrate on the bomb-site, and the director says in voice-over: 'In all my life nothing has quite matched the perfect joy of that moment as my school lay in ruins and the river beckoned with the promise of stolen days.' The idyll that followed was marred when he shot a kingfisher with an airgun and suffered bitter pangs of remorse. Imposing an adult interpretation on the event he comments: 'I became the Fisher King whose wound would not heal until the grail was found and harmony restored.' When the family's uninsured house burned down shortly afterwards he regarded it as a punishment for this sin and for his complicity in his mother's infidelity. Whether that relationship was consummated is not clear, but when Herbert fell mortally ill Ivy nursed him devotedly and made no attempt to disguise her love for him from her husband. Her adolescent son purified himself by a ritual dip in the Thames, believing that if he could swim without causing a single ripple on the surface of the water he would recover the state of grace he had lost. 'That experience, so profound, set me on a quest for images, through cinema, to try and recapture what I knew that day.' At the time of writing, he still swam naked every morning in the cold river that runs past his house in Ireland.

A maverick Salesian teacher, Fr John McGuire, encouraged John to think he might become a writer, but the family's circumstances prevented him from even thinking about going to university. He left school and became an autodidact, scraping a living from a door-to-door dry-cleaning service in partnership with a friend, reading promiscuously and haunting the cinema, while he waited for his call-up to National Service. He wrote articles on spec, a few of which were published by the *Manchester Guardian*, and did some broadcasting. With another friend, Barrie, he formed a Jules-and-Jim three-some with a girl called Pat. One day, in Barrie's absence, he and Pat succumbed to sexual desire, and confessed the deed to Barrie, who was devastated – but only for a few hours, after which he announced that he now realised how shallow and banal Pat was. It was another, comic, re-enactment of the Arthurian triangle.

Boorman's army service was spent mainly in the Education Corps, teaching raw recruits at a Royal Engineers' basic training camp. He was threatened with a court martial for questioning the legitimacy of the Korean War, but charges were dropped when he demonstrated that all his arguments were taken from *The Times*. At about the same time he met a vibrant, attractive young German woman, called Christel, who was working as a nurse in a TB sanatorium. They lived together after his release from the army and, when she became pregnant, married. It was to be a long-lasting and fruitful marriage, though strained by some infidelities on Boorman's part which eventually brought it unhappily to an end. 'Christel had been loyal and true, and I had not. Trust was lost. I lived on suffrance, closely watched. When I finally broke away, the severance was wrenchingly painful for all the family.' But the saddest event in his life so far was the death of his daughter Telsche at the age of thirty-seven, from cancer. She was the eldest of his four children, and collaborated with him on some of his films.

Like many film directors, John Boorman learned his craft in television – not in drama, however, but through editing, directing and producing documentary programmes. He was an early recruit to ITN news, and then joined Southern TV, where he achieved unprecedented success with a regional magazine programme called *Day by Day*. Headhunted by the BBC in Bristol, he caused a stir with a series of films that candidly reflected the changing social mores of Britain in the early 1960s, and he joined a circle of lively young writers in Bristol that included Tom Stoppard, Charles Wood and Peter Nichols. It was collaborating with Peter Nichols on a film about the Dave Clark Five, designed to ride the wave created by the Beatles' *A Hard Day's Night*, that gave Boorman his break in narrative movie-making.

As soon as he was launched into this new career, however, he abandoned the documentary bias of his TV work and exploited the superior technical and budgetary resources of feature films to make works of mythic resonance and – in due course – epic ambition. He was offered the chance to direct a *noir*ish thriller for MGM if Lee Marvin could be persuaded to act in it. Marvin promised to do so on one condition, which he indicated by tossing the script out of the window. Boorman rewrote the script, and filmed the story as if it was a bad dream, shooting each scene in a different dominant colour. When the studio heads saw the rushes they suspected he was insane and interviewed him in the presence of a psychiatrist. But *Point Blank* was a critical success, if not a commercial blockbuster, and in due course, like many of Boorman's productions, became a cult movie.

The autobiography contains a memorable portrait of Lee Marvin, a Hemingwayesque character, incorrigibly macho, haunted by a traumatic combat experience as a Marine in the Second World War, and given to epic binges in which Boorman inevitably became embroiled, leading on one occasion to his being stopped in his car by an LA traffic cop with the immortal question, 'Do you know you have Lee Marvin on your roof?' (He did know.) In 1968 he teamed up with Marvin again to make the aptly named *Hell in the Pacific*, about an American airman and a Japanese naval officer who are washed up together on a tiny desert island in the war. Almost everything that can go wrong with a film went wrong in making this one and Boorman's account is a classic of movie disaster stories.

Hell in the Pacific was not a success at the box office, and neither was its off-beat, experimental successor, *Leo the Last*, though it won the Best Director prize at Cannes. Boorman was approached about making *The Lord of the Rings*, and did a lot of work on it, but the project, like so many film projects, fell through. (He pays a generous tribute to Peter Jackson's eventual realisation of the story.) Boorman's directorial career was beginning to languish: he badly needed a real hit. At this crucial moment he was asked by Warners to consider a novel by James Dickey that they had under option, called *Deliverance*. 'I read the novel with mounting excitement. I knew how to do it.' Of course he did! It was all about a river. Four men take a canoe trip down a fast-moving river in a valley soon to be flooded to make a dam that will provide the electricity for their suburban homes. What starts out as a light-hearted adventure turns into a grim struggle for survival, as the group experiences first the pitiless power of the river and its rapids, and then the malevolence of the 'mountain people' who inhabit the valley's heights. One of the party is drowned, another seriously injured, a third famously sodomised, and the fourth only survives by killing a man with a crossbow. Dickey, who had himself written a script, and retained some right to interfere in the making of the film, meant to celebrate this action as an assertion of manhood; Boorman wanted to end on a more ambiguous note, with the survivor haunted by his deed. Boorman won, but endured some awkward moments with the absurdly pompous Dickey in the process.

Warner were nervous about the prospects of a movie with no woman in it, but it was nominated for three Academy Awards (best film, best director and best editing) and the theme music alone, a simple duet for guitar and banjo conceived by Boorman, earned enough money to put the film into profit. Boorman was now a hot director. He was offered *The Exorcist*, but found the subject repellent and turned it down. Instead he made a didactic fantasy of his own called *Zardoz*, set in a future when developments in medicine have given men and women immortality. In lieu of a fee he took a share of the profits, of which there were none. *Zardoz* flopped. So did his next film, *The Heretic*, intended to be a kind of benign sequel to *The Exorcist*, which infuriated the earlier film's fans, and pleased nobody else. Boorman quotes Pauline Kael against himself: 'It's . . . another in the long history of movie-makers' king-size follies. There's enough visual magic in it for a dozen good movies; what the picture lacks is judgement.' Again Boorman's career was threatened with eclipse, and again he rescued it, this time with *Excalibur*. Though many critics were and continue to be sniffy about that film, it drew enthusiastic audiences world-wide.

And that has been the pattern of Boorman's career as a director – always experimenting, always ambitious, always courting disaster, never afraid of going 'over the top'. He frequently paid the price of failure for his ambition, but invariably bounced back. His imagination thrives on difficulties. He once defined film-making as 'inventing impossible problems for yourself and then failing to solve them'. Many of his films have involved extreme physical risk, discomfort and danger for himself. The reason why the white-water sequences in *Deliverance* are so heart-stoppingly exciting and immediate is that the director himself spent many hours before and during the shoot immersed in the raging river. In preparation for making *The Emerald Forest* he spent weeks living simply with a tribe in the Amazon rainforest, like a scrupulous anthropologist doing fieldwork. It is all part of his self-image as a cinematic Grail knight, prepared to venture into unknown territory in the effort to bring back a transcendent movie.

Adventures of a Suburban Boy is an effortlessly enjoyable read, containing many droll anecdotes which make one laugh out loud, but it is far deeper than the usual show-biz memoir. It is the autobiography of a man who takes himself and his art seriously and writes about both subjects with unusual eloquence and insight. There is an elegiac tone to its concluding section. Boorman ruefully acknowledges changes in movie-making (the digital technology with which one can create astonishing special effects just sitting at a computer console) that have made his kind of physical involvement in the process almost redundant, and reflects wryly that the tyranny of philistine studio executives has been replaced by the tyranny of philistine preview audiences, whose score cards often determine how films are edited and released. Not all the respondents are philistine though. One card he saw said: 'John Boorman's movies are unpredictable, subversive and crazed. Tell him to keep making them no matter what.'

ALAN BENNETT'S SERIAL
AUTOBIOGRAPHY

*U*NTOLD *STORIES*, ALAN Bennett's collection of autobiographical essays, family memoirs, diary extracts and other occasional writings was published in October 2005 to warm and widespread applause in the press, and by the end of February 2006 had sold well over 300,000 copies in hardback. That remarkable figure was achieved partly with the help of some brutal discounting by chain bookstores, online booksellers and supermarkets, of a kind that has destabilised the book trade in the UK and threatens to eliminate independent bookshops. However much one may deplore this phenomenon (and Alan Bennett himself publicly urged readers to buy his book from independents), as an index of popularity the sales figures cannot be gainsaid. Supermarkets know a good loss-leader when they see one. Alan Bennett is undoubtedly one of the most popular writers of recognised literary merit in England.

He first came to fame as one of the brilliant quartet of young Oxbridge graduates (the others being Peter Cook, Dudley Moore and Jonathan Miller) who created and performed *Beyond the Fringe* in 1960 in London, and subsequently in New York, a hugely influential show which may be said to have in some sense inaugurated the 1960s as a decade of youth-driven cultural revolution. (Tony Hendra, for example, has described seeing the revue as a life-changing experience which caused him to abandon his vocation to the Roman Catholic priesthood and to become a satirist instead, moving from England to America to become a founder and contributing editor of the hugely successful American magazine *National Lampoon*.) After *Beyond the Fringe* Bennett gave up the idea of becoming an academic historian and commenced a highly successful career as a playwright, screenplay writer, and occasional actor. *Forty Years On*, *Habeas Corpus*, *Single Spies*, *The Lady in the Van*, *The Madness of George III* and *The History Boys* are among the most acclaimed works of post-war British theatre. The last but one of these was also a much admired feature film, adapted by Bennett (but renamed *The Madness of King George III*, in case American audiences should think it was a sequel to movies called *The Madness of George* and *The Madness of George II* which they had somehow missed). Over the same period he wrote a large number of outstanding television screenplays, including the boldly original 'Talking Heads' for the BBC, a series of extended mono-logues, each delivered straight to camera by a single actor, some of which were later successfully performed on stage. He is, in short, a national treasure, and the popularity of his occasional prose writings, first harvested in the best-selling *Writing Home* (1994) and for a second time in *Untold Stories*, was both a symptom and a confirmation of that status. Together they constitute a kind of serial autobiography, which continues in the selected extracts from his diary published in the *London Review of Books* in the first issue of each new year.

These writings are enjoyed for two reasons in particular: because of what they reveal about the character of the author and because they make you laugh. The two things are connected, for Bennett excels in telling jokes against himself. A typical one in *Untold Stories* concerns a paper he gave to an Oxford historical society on Richard II, the subject of his postgraduate research; at the end he invited questions and after a long silence someone at the back of the room raised a hand and asked, 'Could you tell me where you bought your shoes?' But he also deals with serious, sad, painful experience of a kind which everybody faces sooner or later, like the decline and death of parents, and he does so with a very sure touch.

The first section of *Untold Stories* describes how his mother succumbed to severe depression shortly after she and his father retired to the country cottage they had always dreamed of. Bennett and his father took her to the mental hospital where she was admitted, and returned the same evening to visit her. A medical orderly escorted them to her ward:

He flung open the door on Bedlam, a scene of unimagined wretchedness. What hit you first was the noise. The hospitals I had been in previously were calm and unhurried; voices were hushed; sickness, during visiting hours at least, went hand in hand with decorum. Not here. Crammed with wild and distracted women, lying or lurching about in all the wanton disarray of a Hogarth print, it was a place of terrible tumult. Some of the grey-gowned wild-eyed creatures were weeping, others shouting, while one demented wretch shrieked at short and regular intervals like some tropical bird.

Bennett thinks they must be in the wrong ward, but his father

. . . stopped at the bed of a sad, shrunken woman with wild hair, who cringed back against the pillows.

'Here's your Mam,' he said.

And of course it was only that, by one of the casual cruelties that routine inflicts, she had on admission been bathed, her hair washed and left uncombed and uncurled, so that it now stood out round her head in a mad halo, this straightaway drafting her into the ranks of the demented. Yet the change was so dramatic, the obliteration of her usual self so utter and complete, that to restore her even to an appearance of normality now seemed beyond hope. She was mad because she looked mad.

Dad sat down by the bed and took her hand.

'What have you done to me, Walt?' she said.

'Nay, Lil,' he said and kissed her hand. 'Nay, love.'

And in the kissing and the naming my parents were revealed stripped of all defence. Because they seldom kissed, and though they were the tenderest and most self-sufficient couple, I had never seen my father do anything so intimate as to kiss my mother's hand and seldom since childhood heard them call each other by name. 'Mam' and 'Dad' was what my brother and I called them and what they called each other, their names kept for best. Or worst.

It is hard to imagine that such an experience could be described more movingly and convincingly. The narrator's language is eloquent without being obtrusively literary, vividly evoking the nightmarish scene and its impact on a sensitive unaccustomed observer, but also acting as a foil for the heart-breaking simplicity of the parents' direct speech. There is particular poignancy in Dad's use of the Yorkshire dialect word, 'Nay', now archaic in standard English. Semantically equivalent to 'No', it has a quite different force here, freighted with inarticulate apology, deprecation and dismay.

Although Bennett's mother was soon moved to a more suitable hospital, and in due course recovered from her depression, she succumbed again on several occasions, requiring what her husband described as more 'hospital do's' (ECT and drug treatment) and eventually lapsed into tranquil or tranquillised senility, dying at the age of ninety-one. The hand-kissing motif recurs in Bennett's sardonically self-accusing account of dutiful but unrewarding visits to her nursing home, full of old women waiting to die. He mimics his father's tender gesture, but effectively his mother is already

> . . . dead, or forgotten anyway, living only in the memory of this morose middle-aged man who turns up every fortnight, if she's lucky, and sits there expecting his affection to be deduced from the way he occasionally takes her hand,

stroking the almost transparent skin before putting
it sensitively to his lips.

The significance a kiss can acquire in a family not
normally given to such physical intimacy also appears in
an even darker passage about his father's heart attack,
some twenty years earlier:

> So I sat for a while at his bedside and then stood
> up to say goodbye. And uniquely in my adult-
> hood, kissed him on the cheek. Seeing the kiss
> coming he shifted slightly, and I saw a look of
> distant alarm in his eyes, on account not just of
> the kiss but of what it portended. I was kissing
> him, he clearly thought, because I did not expect
> to see him again. He knew it for what it was,
> and so did I . . . It was the kiss of death.

Of Bennett's two prose collections, *Writing Home* is
probably funnier, but *Untold Stories* is more revealing.
As he tells us in the introduction to the latter, he did
not intend to publish several of the pieces it contains
when he wrote them, but two events caused him to
change his mind. One was being diagnosed with cancer
of the bowel in 1997, and given only a 50 per cent
chance of surviving for more than a year or two, which
made any need to protect his privacy and dignity seem
superfluous, and also generated a fresh stream of intro-
spective writing. Then, when happily he was cured of
the cancer, the appearance a few years later of an
unauthorised biography (*Backing into the Limelight: The
Biography of Alan Bennett*, by Alexander Games) 'made me

press on with my own autobiographical efforts and start thinking of them as pre-posthumous'.

Anyone who has achieved Alan Bennett's level of success in the territory where literature meets show business is axiomatically defined in our culture as a 'celebrity' and must deal with the intrusive interest of the media in his private life which that status brings with it. For most of his professional career Bennett defended his privacy with considerable determination and cunning, deflecting speculation about his sexual orientation by assuming the persona of a celibate bachelor and screening his relationships from public view. When, in 1980, he began to publish extracts from his diary annually in the *London Review of Books*, a feature that soon became an eagerly awaited New Year institution, his friends and companions were usually concealed behind cryptic initials; and when the actor Ian McKellen publicly challenged him to declare whether he was gay, at a charity concert supporting protest against the notorious 'Section 28' of the 1988 Local Government Act, Bennett wittily evaded the question by saying it was like asking someone who had just crawled across the Sahara Desert whether they preferred Malvern or Perrier water.

The diary sequence 1980–90, reprinted from the *LRB* in *Writing Home*, contained several references to doing things in the company of 'A.', but not until near the end was this person identified as female, and that was all the information vouchsafed about her. When Bennett revealed in an interview with Stephen Schiff of *The New Yorker*, published in September 1994, that he had been in a sexual relationship with a woman called Anne Davies for more than a decade, he provoked a feeding frenzy in the British press. She was revealed as the daughter of Hungarian refugees, some ten years younger than Bennett, divorced with three children, whom he had first met when he employed her to clean his London house, and later set up in business running a café next to his country cottage in the village of Clapham, in the Yorkshire Dales, which he had inherited from his parents. According to Alexander Games, Bennett went to ground after the interview appeared, leaving the somewhat puzzled and troubled Anne to field the journalists' questions. *Untold Stories* does not explain why he chose to make their relationship public at this point in time; indeed it contains no direct reference to Anne at all. It does, however, describe other phases of his sexual life with more openness than ever before, and with characteristically droll, self-deprecating humour.

In 1950, when he was sixteen, he came to the conclusion that, 'all things considered', he was homosexual, but his desires then and for some time afterwards were essentially emotional rather than physical and steeped in romantic despair. He was invariably attracted to 'straight' young men who could never reciprocate his feelings, and this seemed to him his inevitable doom. He was unwilling to admit his orientation, least of all to his parents, though they seem to have harboured suspicions. When, as an undergraduate, he tapered his trousers to a fashionably tight narrow fit:

'You can't go out like that,' Mam said. 'People will think you're one of them.'

Whereupon Dad, who was even more shocked than she was, said (and the question must have had a long gestation), 'You're not one of them, are you?'

'Oh Dad,' I think I replied, as if the question was absurd. 'Don't be daft.'

But I never wore the trousers.

The exchange, like many others, later found its way, slightly changed, into the script of a TV play – entitled, *Me, I'm Afraid of Virginia Woolf.*

At the time of *Beyond the Fringe,* he had 'occasional flings, all of them straight, two of them with the same slightly depressing outcomes: shortly after going to bed with me, my partners announce their engagement (to someone else) and are briskly married'. In the next decade he becomes more relaxed about looking for sexual pleasure with men. The ones he falls for are still straight, but 'sex in the seventies is not so particular about gender and boundaries and so I find myself less often rebuffed and even having quite a nice time . . . I also find myself being led back from the paths of deviancy to what becomes, in the eighties anyway, a pretty conventional life'. This is the only, very oblique, allusion to his relationship with Anne Davies in the book. In other places *Untold Stories* describes a happy relationship in recent years with a new partner, Rupert Thomas, the young editor of a design magazine, first mentioned in the diaries as 'R.' in January 1996. So perhaps, consciously or unconsciously, the *New Yorker* interview was a way of bringing the relationship with Anne Davies to an end, even though he paid warm tribute to her there (and according to Games they 'remained extremely close'). Bennett admits that 'homosexuality is a differentness I've

never been prepared wholly to accept in myself'. That
may have complicated his life, but it ensured that he
avoided the sometimes limiting categorisation of 'gay
writer'. In later dramatic work, *The History Boys* and a
play about W.H. Auden, *The Habit of Art*, he 'pushed
the envelope' as regards the explicit and often bawdy
treatment of homosexual behaviour, almost as if he had
decided to test the tolerance of his broadly based audience. Those plays, and the two comic-erotic tales
published in 2011 under the title *Smut: Two unseemly
stories*, one straight and one gay in subject matter, seem
to be part of a late urge to renounce the diffidence and
reticence that characterised Bennett's attitude to sexuality
earlier in life.

Bennett writes very honestly about himself, or he
creates the effect of doing so. He is never vain or preten-
tious, always wryly observant of the weaknesses and
contradictions of his own character, ready to confess to
ignoble or selfish feelings with a candour that sometimes
makes the reader wince. But it is inevitably a selective
self-portrait, a rhetorical construction, that emerges from
these anecdotes, memories and journal entries. He
presents himself as a shy loner at high school, crippled
with self-consciousness about his unusually late puberty
(his voice did not break until well after the age of sixteen,
and the other physical manifestations were equally late
in arriving), and there is no reason to doubt the agonies
of embarrassment and anxiety this caused him. But he
omits to mention that (according to his unofficial biographer) he was much in demand as an actor in school
plays, and particularly praised for his performance as
Kate in *The Taming of the Shrew*, where his unbroken

voice and smooth cheeks would have been an asset. Learning this resolved a paradox which had long puzzled me: how was it that someone who presents himself so convincingly as shy, repressed and awkward could be such a successful actor (and without the benefit of professional training) not only in satirical revue, but later in West End productions of his own plays and in television drama and feature films by other hands? Obviously he used acting, in which a licensed fictional frame is put around behaviour, as a way of overcoming and turning to good account what he perceived as crippling abnormalities and inhibitions in adolescence. Later it was his success as writer and performer in student revue during his postgraduate years at Oxford that catapulted him out of an unpromising start as a medieval historian and into the fame of *Beyond the Fringe*, but he has said very little about that phase of his life – or indeed about the moments of triumph and euphoria that must have been quite frequent in the course of his distinguished professional career. He presents himself for the most part as diffident and depressive, someone who has never entirely freed himself from the psychological shackles of a dim, provincial, lower-middle-class upbringing, and never therefore quite believed in his own success. Hence his delight in relating stories that confirm this pessimistic self-assessment, like the receipt of a complimentary copy of Waterstone's Literary Diary for 1997, in which the birthdays of various contemporary writers are recorded, but the date of his own, 9 May, is blank except for the note, 'The first British self-service launderette is opened on Queensway, London 1949'. Bathos is Bennett's favourite trope.

He was born and brought up in Leeds, but deduces from his date of birth that he was conceived during an August holiday in some cheerless seaside boarding house, imagining his parents' lovemaking constrained by their consciousness of the thin bedroom walls and the adjacency of other guests, 'so much of my timorous and undashing life prefigured in that original circumspect conjunction'. His mother was painfully shy – so much so that she couldn't face her own wedding, and was married privately by a kindly and co-operative clergyman, early enough in the morning for the groom to go punctually to work immediately afterwards. (Reading Bennett's memoirs the Yorkshire proverb 'There's nowt so queer as folk' often comes to mind.) Mr Bennett Sr was a butcher by trade, and eventually had his own shop, but never much enjoyed the occupation. From time to time he entertained various schemes for making money by more enjoyable means, like brewing herbal beer, or becoming a double-bass player in a dance band (he was musical, and played the violin), but they never came to anything. In Alan's memory the little family was resigned to its dullness and marginality when he was growing up, a feeling that 'other people made more of their lives than we did'. Even the Second World War brought no drama into their existence. Mr Bennett was in a reserved occupation and therefore not conscripted; he served as an air-raid warden, but among British industrial cities Leeds suffered relatively little bombing and his duties were light. 'War, peace, it makes no difference, our family never quite joining in, let alone joining up, and the camaraderie passes us by as camaraderie generally did.' Entertainment consisted of listening to the radio, and a twice-weekly visit to the local cinema, whatever was showing; on other evenings his parents retired at nine o'clock to bed, where the schoolboy Alan brought them a cup of tea on returning from his customary solitary walk to the public library.

Mrs Bennett had two sisters, Kathleen and Myra, who were more extrovert, and brought some noise and excitement into the muted Bennett household, though generally to the parents' displeasure and disapproval. Myra used the war to escape the drab confines of Leeds, joined the Women's Auxiliary Air Force and married an RAF serviceman in India. When her husband died Alan witnessed her ill-advised attempt to scatter his ashes on Ilkley Moor on a windy day, remarking 'He didn't want to leave me', as she dusted herself down afterwards. The older sister Kathleen, the dominating and loquacious manageress of a shoe shop, surprised everybody by marrying late in life. But she too was widowed, and succumbed to dementia, which 'unleashes torrents of speech, monologues of continuous anecdote and dizzying complexity, one train of thought switching to another without signal or pause, rattling across points and through junctions at a rate no listener can follow'. Kathleen ends her days in the same mental hospital to which her sister was originally admitted, goes missing and is found in wasteland nearby – dramatically by Alan Bennett himself – dead from exposure.

A dark thread runs through the family history on Bennett's mother's side. After she was admitted to the mental hospital for the first time, his father revealed that her father, Alan's grandfather, committed suicide by drowning. Bennett admits that he was rather excited

by this revelation. 'It made my family more interesting
. . . I had just begun to write but had already given up
on my own background because the material seemed so
thin.' In fact much of his best work was to be distilled
from the memory of what seemed at the time dull ordinary
experience, and like most writers he suffers occasional
qualms of conscience about exploiting his nearest and
dearest in this way. Bennett's uneasiness about his last
encounter with his father (described above) was
compounded by the circumstance that he had just written
a television play, then in pre-production, about a man
who has a heart attack on the beach at Morecambe, the
same beach where Bennett's own parents took their last
walk together, making him feel that in some uncanny
way he had caused his father's death. Six years later he
returned to the same emotional nexus, another TV play
about a man who visits his father in intensive care to be
with him when he dies, but is in bed with a nurse at the
crucial moment.

Bennett has based several of his female characters on
his mother and recalls a remark of hers, 'By, you've had
some script out of me!' which obviously struck home.
But typically he explored its implications creatively in a
different context – the play he wrote about Miss Shepherd, *The Lady in the Van*. This was based on one of
the more bizarre episodes in Alan Bennett's life, when
he allowed a crazed, filthy, smelly, aggressive, bigoted
vagrant of genteel origins to live in an insanitary camper
parked in the front garden of his London house for
fifteen years. Why did he put up with her, and for so
long? Altruistic compassion alone cannot explain it.
Perhaps, as some lines in the play suggest, he was

compensating for guilt at neglecting his mother in illness
and old age (for though he visited her regularly, it was
often with impatience and ill-grace) by being kind to
the ungrateful Miss Shepherd, who did not take him
away from his metropolitan life. Almost certainly he felt
from an early stage of their acquaintance that she would
make interesting copy. He made several attempts to write
a play about their relationship, but significantly it was
only when he split his own character into two dramatis
personae – Bennett the decent private individual, exasperated by the demands of his ungrateful tenant, but
unable to extricate himself from her toils, and Bennett
the anarchic, ego-driven writer fascinated by her extraordinary character and outrageously transgressive behaviour
– that the play took off, and became a kind of parable
of the way writers turn life into art.

Bennett is gratefully aware that, 'For a writer nothing
is ever quite as bad as it is for other people because,
however dreadful, it may be of use'. This is well illus-
trated by the account of his treatment for cancer, 'An
Average Rock Bun' (the title refers to the size of his
tumour), and by an alarming story of being the victim
of an unprovoked homophobic attack in a small Italian
town. In both pieces he manages to find humour in
even the grimmest circumstances, and avoids any hint
of self-pity or self-dramatisation. The same scrupulous
honesty characterises his treatment of more trivial plights
and dilemmas. He declines an honorary degree at Oxford
in protest against the university's recent acceptance of
an endowment from Rupert Murdoch, but then wonders
if he hasn't 'slightly made a fool of myself', thus denying
himself any satisfaction from the gesture. He analyses in

exquisite and amusing detail the reasons why he declined
a knighthood, but adds 'lest it be thought that this refusal
has much to do with modesty, when the list of those
who had turned down honours was leaked in the newspapers I cared enough to note (I hope wryly) how
obscurely placed I was on the list and that sometimes I
wasn't even mentioned at all'. But even Bennett's
candour has its limits. 'I hope wryly' – if he doesn't
know, who does?

When Bennett left school he was a practising Anglican,
nurturing vague ideas of becoming a minister, and politically conservative. Now he seems to have no religious
belief and supports the left on most political issues, but
he enjoys visiting old churches, cathedrals and ruined
abbeys, about which he is knowledgeable, and admits
that the destruction of stained glass and statuary at the
Reformation still moves him to more indignation than
recent atrocities committed in the former Yugoslavia or
Sierra Leone. His socialism too is personal and nostalgic
rather than ideological. The only time he voted Conservative was when a Labour government threatened to
extend the motorway network – a bad move, since the
Tories have been much more enthusiastic supporters of
motorised transport, at the expense of railways and the
English countryside. Because he benefited from free
university education himself Bennett opposes the introduction of tuition fees, refusing to take into account that
quite different socio-economic conditions now obtain.
(In his day – and mine – only 5 per cent of the age
group got a university education, so the state could afford

to educate those lucky few for free, whether they needed the subsidy or not; now it's about 40 per cent.) His opposition to the war in Iraq is unqualified, and strongly felt, but not really argued. When the news of Saddam Hussein's arrest breaks, he notes in his diary, 15 December 2003: 'Whatever is said it does not affect the issue. We should not have gone to war. It has been a shameful year.'

Some readers, especially American ones, may find the diary entry for 11 September 2001 somewhat perfunctory. It reads in its entirety:

> Working rather disconsolately when Tom M. rings to tell me to switch on the television as the Twin Towers have been attacked. Not long after I switch on one of the towers collapses, an unbearable sight, like a huge plumed beast plunging earthwards. I go to put the kettle on and in that moment the other tower collapses.

It seems surprising that there is no reflection here, or in the days that follow, on the significance of the event, no speculation about what fanatical conviction and chilling indifference to death drove the perpetrators of this unimaginable deed, no sense that possibly the human world had changed for ever in consequence. It is of course possible that Bennett wrote about all these things but decided his thoughts would seem redundant when reproduced much later. That is the danger of publishing a diary: leave it unedited and you risk being boring; edit it and you may leave a misleading impression. The characteristic bathos of missing the collapse of the second tower while going to make a cup of tea seems out of place here, and the 'plumed beast' simile neglects the human suffering involved. But it's a rare and uncharacteristic lapse of judgement. The fact is that Alan Bennett is more at ease with the homely, the private, even the trivial than he is with big historical ideas and epic events. Again and again in this book he demonstrates that almost anything that happens to a person can be interesting, moving and entertaining if you write about it well enough.

THE GREENE MAN WITHIN

T HE BOOK* BEGINS:

I was standing by the window in the Plaza Hotel, looking out. Below – ten stories below – I could make out round-faced women in ponchos standing on the sidewalk of the city named for peace and renting out cellphones to passersby. At their sides, sisters (or could it be daughters?) were sitting on mountainous piles of books, mostly advising pedestrians on how to win a million dollars. Along the flower-bordered strip of green that cuts through Bolivia's largest metropolis, a soldier was leading his little girl by the hand, pointing out Mickey and Minnie in Santa's sleigh.

The scene is described by synecdoche – parts which stand for the whole – as it has to be in this kind of writing. The art is in the selection of details and the way they surprise and inform us. The default associations of 'Plaza Hotel' for a reader in America, where the book was first published, would be New York, but the

* Pico Iyer, *The Man Within My Head* (2012).

round-faced women in ponchos immediately establish an exotic context. It is, however, a complex exoticism, in which the local and the traditional co-exist with the international and the modern, generating for the observant visitor ironic incongruities of which the native inhabit-ants, with different priorities, are unaware. Even if one didn't already know from the book's jacket-copy that the man within Pico Iyer's head is Graham Greene, one might guess that he had learned from that writer how to evoke a foreign place (in this case, La Paz, Bolivia). Compare, for instance, the opening paragraph of *The Heart of the Matter*:

> Wilson sat on the balcony of the Bedford Hotel with his bald pink knees thrust against the iron-work. It was Sunday and the Cathedral bell clanged for matins. On the other side of Bond Street, in the windows of the High School, sat the young negresses in dark blue gym-smocks engaged on the interminable task of trying to wave their wire-spring hair.

Greene's style is not, however, an influence Iyer mentions in this book; his acknowledged debts to the novelist are more existential.

Enervated by the high altitude, he draws the curtain on the hotel window and sleeps for a while, waking with an irresistible urge to write, though he has come to Bolivia to take a break from writing. He writes 'unstoppably . . . the words came out of me as if someone (something) had a message urgently to convey'. What he writes is a sketch of a boy standing at the dormitory window of a British boarding school, watching as the 'last parental car' drives away at the commencement of a new term, calculating the number of institutional weeks and days ahead, 'trying to magick the numbers down', and listening to the other boys sniffling under their covers. The writer stares at his work, 'as if it were something I'd found rather than composed. I'd been at a school akin to this thirty years before – the emotions weren't entirely foreign to me – but why was the main character . . . called "Greene", as if he had something to do with the long-dead English novelist?' Interrupted, as he ponders this question, by a waiter wordlessly bringing a tank of oxygen to the door of his room (a deft touch of local colour Greene would have approved) the writer then wonders why that morning he had remembered his father 'eyes alight and unfailingly magnetic', laughing uproariously when watching *The Sound of Music*, and himself laughing at exactly the same point in the movie forty years later. 'I looked down again and saw the name in my handwriting: "Greene." The novelist had never even come to Bolivia, as far as I knew. Was it only through another that I could begin to get at myself?' The next section begins: 'I drew back the curtain and, as the light came in, recalled the same thing had happened three years before, pretty much to the day.' He had taken his mother on a trip to Easter Island, where he wrote a story about a Catholic missionary priest that was almost parodically derivative from Graham Greene.

In these opening pages Pico Iyer establishes the basic themes of his book, and its narrative method: being in one place triggers the memory of another place and then

another memory, a series of memories which he inter-
prets through the 'familiar compound ghost' (T.S. Eliot's
phrase in 'Little Gidding' seems appropriate) of Graham
Greene and his characters, as he seeks an authentic sense
of his own identity. The next morning he makes an
excursion to Lake Titicaca on the Bolivia/Peru border.
'As the bus, groaning and faltering, began to sputter out
of town, the other great presence of my life came back
to me again.' This is his father, recalled making a surprise
visit to his son at an Oxford college, barely giving the
latter's current girlfriend time to slither out of a back
window. 'As he walked into the room . . . my father
might have been walking into his own vanished youth,
twenty-six years before; he had arrived from Bombay
and been given a prize room in the ancient cloisters.'

On the bus he notices a woman in her late thirties
stealing glances at him, and she introduces herself as the
guide he had requested. As she questions him about his
life he registers her envy of his freedom and mobility.
'I'd found this theme echoed in every page of Graham
Greene: the foreigner, precisely by going to another
country, brings a whiff of a different world into the lives
of the locals he meets.' They get on well in the course
of the day, to the point where she ventures to give him
a neck massage during a boat trip on the lake. The
possibility of further intimacy hovers in the air, but he
has a wife in Japan, she has two children which his fee
will help to feed, and the moment passes. Pico Iyer
records several such encounters in the course of his
itinerant life – one young woman who caught his eye
on a street in Nicaragua asked him to marry her within
five minutes – and they are all connected in his mind

with the figure of Phuong, the Vietnamese mistress of the narrator in Greene's 'archetypal novel', *The Quiet American*.

The Man Within My Head (a title which echoes that of Greene's first novel, *The Man Within*) is not an easy book to categorise, or to read, because it is a memoir that deliberately renounces chronological structure, shifting abruptly from one time and place to another like a stream-of-consciousness novel. 'I remember walking into a long-distance telephone parlor in the Mexican town of Mérida one hot August afternoon . . .' 'I was in Saigon one autumn, and had just checked into the hotel Majestic . . .' 'We were driving . . . down unpaved roads across the highlands of Ethiopia . . .' These are typical opening sentences of the short sections into which the chapters are divided. The globe spins back and forth dizzyingly as one reads, the episodes are rarely tied to particular dates, and they come in a seemingly random order. Facts that would help us to follow a particular story are revealed much later – or not at all. This frag-mentary, allusive, jumbled narrative method is of course motivated. One reason is stated: 'like Greene, I suspect, I'd never had much time for memoir: it was too easy to make yourself the center – even the hero – of your story and use recollection as a way to forgive yourself for everything . . . to soothe the rush of often contra-dictory and inexplicable events in every life into a kind of pattern and even a happy, redemptive ending.' Another, unstated reason is that the absence of chrono-logical order foregrounds theme: Graham Greene as guru,

guide and father-substitute in the writer's quest for
self-understanding.

One has, however, a tendency to make sense of
individual lives in chronological terms, and I found myself,
as I read the book, mentally constructing the outline of a
conventional biography from the sparse and erratically
supplied information about Pico Iyer and his family, supplemented by occasional recourse to the internet. He is the
only offspring of two Indian scholars, the philosopher and
theosophist Raghavan N. Iyer and the comparative reli-
gionist Nandini Nanak Mehta, born in 1957, two years
after his father arrived in Oxford on a scholarship, and
became in due course a Fellow of St Anthony's College.
When Pico (named after Giovanni Pico della Mirandola,
a neo-Platonist philosopher of the Italian Renaissance) was
eight, and attending the famous Dragon prep school, his
father accepted a post at the University of California in
Santa Barbara, and bought a house in the foothills way out
of town. For Raghavan, it was a good move. He was a
charismatic teacher and thinker whose mixture of political
radicalism and oriental mysticism made him a campus star
in the ideological climate of the 1960s. The young boy,
however, who had always thought of himself as English,
felt uprooted and alienated. Every morning a bus made an
hour-long circuit round the canyons before depositing him
at a school where his abilities placed him among students
who were two years older and had very different interests.
He calculated that due to the strength of the dollar against
the pound, he could fly back and forth to England three
times a year and be a boarder at the Dragon school for
less than the annual cost of his school bus fare. Improbable
as that sounds, his parents agreed to let him go.

The mature Pico's comment, 'A curious decision, perhaps, for a boy of nine', seems a monumental under-statement. It invites interpretation as the son's rejection of the father's dominating presence, and a determination to succeed on his own terms. In retrospect we understand why, with no logical connection, a memory of the father followed quickly on the vignette of the schoolboy called Greene in the opening pages, and that the fictional boy's feeling of desertion puzzled the writer because it had no equivalent in his own experience – he *chose* that kind of education and flourished on it. From the Dragon he won a scholarship to Eton (described but not named in the book) and from there another scholarship to Oxford, and then yet another to Harvard, where he taught for a couple of years before joining *Time* magazine in 1982 and becoming a successful, much travelled journalist and essayist, and in the last decade the author of several books, one of them entitled *The Global Soul: Jet Lag, Shopping Malls and the Search for Home*. He seems to refer to it when he recalls 'In Toronto, one hot summer . . . I spoke about the new possibilities of our global order, and the way it allowed for multiple homes and multiple selves'.

From an early age, then, Pico Iyer shared with Graham Greene a low opinion of home and an addic-tion to travel. But he had a parental home in California to which he returned regularly as a student, and this cultural commuting felt like 'moving through some alle-gory between a City of Hope where history has been abolished, and a City of History, where hope can be slipped in only as contraband'. That eloquent image explains why *The Quiet American* was a key book for him: its narrator an 'Unquiet Englishman', a cynical, world-weary journalist in Vietnam who befriends, opposes and finally defeats, in both love and war, the idealistic but dangerously blinkered Yank, and is left burdened with guilt, 'wishing there was someone to whom I could say I was sorry'. Privileging *The Quiet American* produces a somewhat distorted version of Greene's *oeuvre*, making the later fiction seem more representative, and of higher quality, than it actually was, and leading to some dubious generalisations like 'He could never quite bring himself to believe in God'. The man who wrote *The Power and the Glory*, *The Heart of the Matter* and *The End of the Affair* surely believed in God at the time in any ordinary sense of that formula, and the change in the novels from *The Quiet American* onwards to a sceptical, doubting 'implied author' makes that all the more obvious.

Iyer was never a believer, but he became increasingly interested in religion. He writes a book about the Dalai Lama and a novel about Islam. He goes to stay in a Catholic monastery in California, and almost at once begins to write as he did in the hotel room in La Paz: 'words poured out of me, in spite of me, pages of them . . . Words of radiance and affirmation that might have come from some unfallen self within me that I'd forgotten.' These moments – there are several of them in the book – when the writer describes composition as a spontaneous event scarcely under conscious control are reminiscent of first-person descriptions of conversion and mystical rapture in William James's *Varieties of Religious Experience*, and they invariably have some association with Greene. The earliest, seminal one seems to have happened in the late 1980s. Bored in Bhutan one afternoon, on some travel-journalism assignment, Pico Iyer begins to read a copy of *The Comedians* he brought with him, at first idly and then, as light fades outside his hotel room, with increasing absorption. 'Something strange began to happen. I felt as if I was on the inside of the book, a spotlight trained on something deep inside me.' Just at that moment the real lights go out because of a power cut. He turns on the gas fire and continues to read, crouched on the floor, by its orange glow, and when he has finished the book he feels a compulsion to write a response to its author on sheets of the hotel notepaper. 'Out it all came, like a confession and an essay all at once: everything the novel had made me feel as it pinned me against the wall and asked the cost of watching from the sidelines.' It's a pity that the sequence ends with those two tired clichés because it describes a crucial event, a kind of conversion. Next day he mailed the letter to Graham Greene, and returned to the 'usual dinners and distractions' of his social life. 'But something in me had turned, and I realised that wit or clever observation would never be enough.'

Iyer knew Greene's address in Antibes by heart although he had never written to the novelist before, nor tried to visit him there. He had read too many reports by others who had done so, and retired baffled by the affable but inscrutable persona Greene presented to them, to risk a disillusioning encounter with his hero. But a few months after sending his letter, having received no reply, he wrote another, offering to write a profile of Greene in the unlikely event that 'he wanted to explain himself to *Time* magazine'. Greene replied courteously that 'if any letter could make him succumb, it would be

mine . . . But time was short now, and he had much to
do.' A year and a half later, the novelist was dead. One
can work out that it was in these years – late 1980s, early
1990s – that Pico Iyer met his wife Hiroko, saw the
family house in California burned down by terrifying
bush fires, and 'decided to make my sense of belonging
truly internal and go to the most clarifying society I
knew, Japan, to live in a two-room flat with little on its
shelves but a worn copy of *The Quiet American*'. It sounds
like an ending – this quasi-monastic withdrawal into a
simple, austere way of life in provincial Japan, with *The
Quiet American* as secular scripture – but that's an illusion
created by the absence of dates, for Pico Iyer continued
to travel widely, and to interrogate himself.

'As I went back and forth, in my life and then in my
head,' he observes, 'I came to see how much it was a
story, in the end, of fathers and sons.' The boy Greene
was unhappy at Berkhamsted school because his father
was its headmaster, making him the target of suspicion
and bullying by the other pupils – unhappy enough to
run away and sleep rough on the local Common for
several days, a microcosm of his future life. Young Pico
was happy at the Dragon school but had chosen it to get
away from his father's dominating, extrovert personality,
and in later life adopted Greene as his spiritual father. 'At
heart he offered me a way of looking at things, and the
way one looked became a kind of theology.' The publication of the second volume of Norman Sherry's authorised
biography in 1994 prompted Iyer to make Greene the
subject of one of his *Time* essays, and shortly afterwards
he picked up a recorded phone message from his father
which seemed to be about the article but dissolved into

helpless sobbing. 'Something had obviously touched him, or devastated him, in the Greeneian theme of being unable to look anywhere but to oneself for blame.' When they next met Pico thought he saw the pain of this realisation in his father's eyes, but no explanation or reconciliation took place before Raghavan died a few weeks later after a short illness.

'You really want to spend all this time with Graham Greene?' Hiroko asks her husband. Her puzzlement is understandable, and will be felt to some degree by many readers of this book. Most of us have felt at different times of our lives a special kinship with a writer, and interpreted our lives in the light of his or her imagination, but seldom for so long, or so obsessively, as Pico Iyer. His excitement at finding some trivial connection between his life and Greene's – for instance, reading the epigraph to Greene's *Monsignor Quixote* shortly after the Dalai Lama quoted the same lines from *Hamlet* in conversation with him, or when he 'shuddered' at discovering that his father's hero Gandhi was born on the same day, thirty years earlier, as Greene – can seem excessive, almost superstitious. Nevertheless this is a courageous, intriguing book, perhaps better described generically not as a memoir but a confession, of someone whose education and profession made him a privileged citizen of the whole modern world, but who found globalisation spiritually unsatisfying. If it seems obsessive, Pico Iyer could cite in self-defence Graham Greene's observation, in his essay on Walter de la Mare: 'Every creative writer worth our consideration . . . is a victim: a man given over to an obsession.' But one can't help hoping that he has got Graham Greene out of his system with this book, and will produce more writing like the episode near the end, vividly describing an alarming car accident and its aftermath in a remote part of Bolivia, which has no reference to the English writer, and owes nothing to him − except perhaps in style and story-telling.

SIMON GRAY'S DIARIES

*S*IMON GRAY, WHO *died suddenly in August 2008 –
why do I say 'suddenly', implying that his death was
unexpected, when as he knew, and all the world knew, all
his readers anyway, he had been suffering from several life-
threatening maladies for years, including prostate cancer, of
which his doctor said that there was no point in worrying
about it since he would almost certainly die of one of the other
things that were wrong with him before the prostate cancer
could kill him, which turned out to be true – and yet it was
sudden, his death, even if not unexpected, which is not quite
the same as expected, and was a shock to his friends, to me
anyway, who counted myself among them, though not a close
one.*

Thus might Simon Gray himself have begun this
essay, in the late style of his own diaries, a free-flowing
stream of report and reminiscence which perpetually
eddies back to question its own accuracy and authenticity. I first met him when I was Henfield Writing
Fellow at the University of East Anglia in the summer
term of 1977. One of my duties was inviting other
writers to come and talk about their work, and having
greatly enjoyed his plays *Butley*, and *Otherwise Engaged*,
and others written for television, I invited him. Gray
was at that time combining his playwriting career with

a lectureship in the English Department of Queen Mary College London, and I thought that he might, like myself, find it easier to talk about his creative work away from his academic home. Anyway he accepted, and arrived at my accommodation on the campus grasping a bottle of malt whisky, which was empty when he left the next morning. Perhaps because of the whisky, though he drank most of it, I don't have a very detailed memory of his visit. It was agreeable enough, but no instant bonding occurred. He struck me as being either shy or guarded, I couldn't decide which, and he had not at that date started publishing his very unguarded diaries.

We met occasionally after that, usually by accident – in a theatre bar, on a West End pavement, at a literary festival in Toronto – but exchanged mutually complimentary notes about each other's work from time to time, more frequently in later years. In the summer of 2007 we realised a long-mooted plan to have dinner together with our wives in London, but Simon and Victoria seemed subdued that evening (with good reason – I learned later he had just been diagnosed as having lung cancer) and the background noise in the crowded restaurant was trying to my imperfect hearing, so it was a slightly disappointing evening. The last postcard I received from Simon, in the following year, urged that we should repeat the occasion in a more sympathetic venue. A few weeks later, before I could follow up the suggestion, he was dead.

It was, then, a tenuous relationship in terms of personal contact, and yet through the diaries I, for my part at least, acquired a sense of shared intimacy with

Simon Gray. From the very first one, *An Unnatural Pursuit* (1985), I was a devotee of these books, buying them as soon as they appeared, and finishing them with a sigh of regret, having devoured them with the kind of trance-like pleasure that I associate with childhood reading, rather than the analytical attention of the professional critic. Rereading them after his death for the purpose of writing this tribute was enormously enjoyable, not least for the renewed laughter they provoked; but I was also made aware of their evolution into a wholly original style of journal-writing, and of their increasingly confessional nature.

An Unnatural Pursuit and its successor, *How's That For Telling 'Em, Fat Lady?* (1988), were both written during, and mostly about, the production of a play – in fact the same play, *The Common Pursuit* (1984), a key work in Gray's *oeuvre*. The title is that of a well-known collection of essays by F.R. Leavis, who took it in his turn from T.S. Eliot's definition of the aim of literary criticism, 'the common pursuit of true judgment'. It was to sit at the feet of Leavis that young Gray went to Cambridge to read English, and he stayed on there for many years as a postgraduate and part-time tutor, though not a devout Leavisite. (Gray's complex relationship to Leavis and his position in the Cambridge English Faculty is wittily and frankly anatomised in two essays appended to *An Unnatural Pursuit*.) The title of the play may also echo Thomas Jefferson's phrase, 'the pursuit of happiness', for it is about a group of Cambridge graduates, five men and one woman, who fail to fulfil their promise or their hopes through a combination of circumstance and character.

The first scene shows them as students involved in the publication of a literary magazine of which one of them is the editor (a character based on Gray's friend, the poet and critic Ian Hamilton); the second and third show him struggling with the same task nine years later in the real world of publishing, variously helped and hindered by the others; and the fourth and final scene poignantly returns them, by means of a revolve, to the hopeful high spirits of the opening scene.

Someone who had read an amusingly candid article of Gray's called 'Flops and Other Fragments' published in 1982 suggested that he should keep a diary of his next production, and that was how *An Unnatural Pursuit* and all its successors came into existence. He recorded notes on the progress of *The Common Pursuit* almost daily on a tape recorder, and lightly edited the resulting transcripts, adding corrections and afterthoughts in footnotes. The diary begins on 25 November 1983 when, after working through the night, fuelled by cigarettes and malt whisky, he 'finishes' the play, i.e. finishes a draft with which he is sufficiently satisfied to try and get it performed. 'This, for me, is the only moment of pure happiness I ever experience in the playwriting business,' he notes, well aware that the path to production is never a smooth one, especially in the commercial theatre where he mainly worked. Of all the diaries this is the one most fully focused on a single play, and I know of no better account of the highs and lows, the suspense, frustration, elation, and volatile personal interaction, involved in putting on a play, as seen from the writer's point of view. Finding a producer, finding a director, finding a theatre, casting the play, developing and revising the play in rehearsal, showing it to an audience for the first time, showing it to the critics at press night, waiting to see if it is going to be a hit or a flop: every stage in the process is fraught with potential euphoria or despair.

In this case only the attachment of a director was unproblematic. Harold Pinter, who had directed several of Simon's previous plays, liked *The Common Pursuit* and was willing to direct. Surprisingly, nowhere in the diaries does the playwright explain how they first became friends and collaborators, but it was the most important relationship in his professional life – and perhaps in his personal life too, outside his family. In background and character they were very different, as were their plays – but this was probably the foundation of their partnership. Pinter wouldn't have wanted to direct imitations of his own distinctive and innovative form of drama, but he appreciated the wit and crafts-manship of Gray's plays and enjoyed bringing them to life on the stage.

The stage in this case was the Lyric, Hammersmith, from which they hoped to transfer the play, if it was successful, to the West End. It pleased its audiences, and a majority of the critics, but the project failed for lack of a theatre and because of some treachery, Gray thought, on the part of the producers. The story ends with an emotional and rather drunken dinner party for the cast after the last performance at the Lyric, at which Pinter and Gray get into a furious argument based on a mutual misunderstanding, and the latter concludes: 'Perhaps the problem with keeping a diary, and the reason I'll never keep another one, is that one records only the things one would prefer to forget.' Fortunately for us he did not keep this resolution.

An Unnatural Pursuit contains many slyly amusing asides (as when Pinter blames a hangover on the dyspeptic effects of white wine, and Gray comments, 'I've observed that quite a few people, amongst them myself, consider that white wine is an alternative to alcohol, which is probably a mistake') but no hilarious comic set-pieces like those in its sequel, *How's That For Telling 'Em, Fat Lady?* Its title is the punch line of a joke which has no particular relevance to the narrative. Subtitled *A Short Life in the American Theatre*, it tells the story, by the same tape-recorded method as before, of Gray's participation in American productions of two of his plays, *The Common Pursuit* in Los Angeles, and *Dog Days* in Dallas, Texas.

The Matrix in Los Angeles is a tiny theatre with only ninety-nine seats, which exempts it from Equity regulations. The actors and director and designers are unpaid because they are unemployed and would rather work for nothing than do nothing, while Simon Gray 'will go anywhere, and do anything' to get one of his plays produced, especially *The Common Pursuit*, and hopes this production might lead to one in New York. The disproportion between the small scale of the event and the immense amount of anxiety, conflict and paranoia it generates among those involved is one source of the comedy. Another is the persona of the homesick dramatist himself, who experiences as much 'irritation, exhaustion, frustration' outside the theatre as inside it. His baffled encounters with Californians in the most ordinary situations constantly illustrate the adage that England and America are two countries divided by a common language. Though living in the world capital of the movie industry he is unable to rent a VCR machine that works, a farcical saga that goes on for days and weeks. In Dallas, a wasteland of freeways and parking lots, punctuated by tower blocks whose glazed and exposed elevators give him vertigo, his only means of escape from a female interviewer made drunkenly libidinous by the champagne he orders is to allow her to drive him to a quickly invented appointment at the theatre, a vividly described journey 'that in real time lasted only fifteen minutes, but in true time lasted a couple of months, to be deducted in due course, no doubt, from my account'. All the while Gray himself is consuming amazing quantities of booze – malt whisky at night and champagne by day from breakfast onwards. He does, however, give up smoking, by chewing nicotine gum in such quantities that he has permanent indigestion. The theatrical story for once has a happy ending – *The Common Pursuit* gets to New York and is a hit – but not before a crisis in one of the previews drives him to buy a pack of cigarettes. 'I smoked my way through them, one after the other and sometimes probably two simultaneously, and felt – I suppose this is the worst part – such joy, such release to have the murderous old friend swirling about in the lungs again.'

It is likely that Gray was genetically disposed to these addictions. We learn from later diaries that his mother, though an Olympic athlete in youth, was a heavy smoker who died of lung cancer at fifty-nine, and his beloved younger brother Piers died of alcoholism at the age of forty-nine. The high stress level of Simon's chosen profession (itself a kind of psychological addiction, as he was well aware) did not make it any easier for him to kick these habits, and their effects become an increasingly grim motif threaded through the comic reportage and ironic introspection of the diaries.

The Common Pursuit did eventually make it to the West End in 1988, where it had a successful run with a cast of young actors who had achieved celebrity via stand-up comedy and television, notably Stephen Fry and Rik Mayall, and it was through this connection that in 1995 these two actors were cast to play the leading roles in *Cell Mates*, which Gray himself directed, a play about the convicted spy George Blake and Sean Bourke, the petty criminal who helped him escape from Wormwood Scrubs. This production created a front-page news story when Fry disappeared two days after the opening night, leaving on his answerphone the cryptic message, 'I'm sorry. I'm so very sorry.' At first it was feared that he might have committed suicide, but in due course he turned up in Bruges, having suffered a catastrophic attack of stage fright apparently triggered by an unkind review of his performance.

Simon Gray told the story from his point of view in *Fat Chance*, published later that year. Although it belongs thematically with the previous diaries, it is not written in diary form. Nor was it dictated, a method which tends to string clauses together in a manner that resembles casual speech. *Fat Chance* is very much a *written* book, with a more complex syntax and temporal structure than its predecessors. The narrative shifts backwards and forwards in time to bring out foreshadowings of the disaster being prepared by fate for the unwitting playwright. 'A very obscure place, the future. But let us dip quickly into it now, to when it's become the past, to get it over with . . . there was far worse to come . . .' That is a representative quote. It is hard to say which was worst for Gray – learning of the disappearance of his lead actor hours after he had been told the play was going to be a box-office hit, or the failure of heroic efforts to rescue it with a replacement actor, or the fact that the media unjustly attributed Fry's breakdown to the quality of the play, making Gray responsible for the whole debacle. The playwright made public statements at the time which he later regretted, but *Fat Chance* is a powerful expression of controlled anger.

Enter a Fox (2001) reverts to the diary form, but in a new key. Gray ruminates wryly on the fate of his recent play *The Late Middle Classes*, which failed to move from its first production outside London to the West End although it was later revealed that the judges of the Evening Standard Theatre Awards would probably have given it the prize for Best Play if it had; confesses he is blocked on his work in progress; wonders if in fact he has another play in him; refers to a fairly recent emergency operation which removed 'a yard or so' of his intestine and obliged him to give up drinking (which of course has made him even more dependent on smoking); records symptoms of increasing general debility; and describes the rather aimless repetitive routine, almost like a Beckett character's, of his daily life. The diary is written, not dictated, but it sounds as if it is spoken, or as if Gray is speaking to himself, an interior monologue. It was a prose style which he further developed into a brilliantly effective instrument of self-expression in the acclaimed sequence of books referred to collectively by the title of the first of them, *The Smoking Diaries*, which brought him a new and wider audience in his later years. They are available on DVDs, very well read by the author himself, and there is no better way to enjoy them.

The first volume, published in 2004, begins with the author attaining the age of senior citizenship, entitling him, he hopes, to

> . . . a respectful attention when I speak, unfailing assistance when I stumble or lurch, and absence of registration when I do the things I've been doing more and more frequently recently, but have struggled to keep under wraps – belching, farting, dribbling, wheezing . . . Thus am I, at sixty-five and a day. Thus he is at sixty-five and a day, a farter, a belcher, a dribbler, and a what else did I say I did, farting, belching, dribbling, oh yes, wheezing. But then as I smoke something like sixty-five cigarettes a day people are likely to continue with their inevitable 'Well, if you insist on getting through three packets, etc.' to which I will reply, as always – actually I can't remember what I always reply, and how could I, when I don't believe anyone, even my doctors, ever says anything like, 'Well, if you will insist, etc.' In fact, I'm merely reporting a conversation I have with myself, quite often, when I find myself wheezing my way not only up but down the

stairs, and when I recover from dizzy spells after pulling on my socks, tying up my shoelaces, two very distinct acts.

Classical rhetoricians had a catalogue of technical terms for the ways in which Gray incorporates into his text his false starts, mistakes, repetitions, digressions and self-critical reflections, instead of deleting or emending them as good prose normally requires, but you don't have to know your *apoplanesis* from your *aposiopesis* to appreciate the effects of such tropes: spontaneity, comedy, honesty. It's a style that reminds one occasionally of Sterne's *Tristram Shandy* and modernist stream-of-consciousness novels, but it is quite uniquely Gray's, the verbal manifestation of the man himself, unprotected by any fictional mask, naked and quite frequently ashamed.

Always we are made conscious of the act of writing itself. Typically Gray begins a sequence by describing himself sitting in his study, or at a favourite table in a Barbados beach hotel, or on a terrace in Spetses, writing with a ballpoint on a yellow legal pad, and of course smoking, usually alone in the small hours, but sometimes in the midst of other people whom he describes and eavesdrops on, before dredging up some memory from the past. Always the prose seems inseparable from the meandering train of thought it articulates, and at one point in the second volume of the series, *The Year of the Jouncer*, Gray actually declares that he will never revise anything in future: 'you are only what you write, never what you rewrite.' Even if he kept this resolution to the letter (which I doubt) he eventually discovered for himself the deconstructionist catch-22: 'as soon as

I've written a sentence I've already changed my life, or at least added to it, so that it's impossible ever to catch myself up into a state of completeness.' Nevertheless he narrowed the gap to as fine a point as any writer I can think of.

Julian Barnes described *The Smoking Diaries* as 'the funniest book I've read all year', and Philip Hensher as 'one of the funniest books I have ever read in my life'. It is indeed laugh-out-loud funny at many points, as are its sequels, *The Year of the Jouncer* (2006) and *The Last Cigarette* (2008), though it is hard to illustrate this quality without impracticably long quotation, since so much of the humour depends upon context and timing – the unexpected qualification, or the subtly delayed punch line to an extended anecdote, like the theatrical horror-story in *The Year of the Jouncer* about a drunken director who completely wrecks a production of one of Gray's plays, concluding with the revelation that the director was Gray himself. He had a gift for exploiting the comic possibilities of more ordinary experiences, like travel and tourism, which makes a journey to Spetses via Athens in *The Last Cigarette* into a hilarious epic of frustration, discomfort and humiliation. Yes, these books are very funny, and will always be read for the liberating laughter they provoke. But rereading them in the shadow of Simon's death I was struck by how dark they are too, how insistent is the underlying note of self-loathing and despair. 'God, I hate myself' he mentally exclaims early in *The Smoking Diaries*, and it is a note that is sounded with increasing frequency in these books. He became his own severest critic and judge.

From the memories, some of them revisited several

times, a kind of autobiography emerges. Gray and his older brother were taken to Montreal at the beginning of the Second World War when they were three and four years old, and left there with their grandparents by their mother, who one day said she was going out for some milk and didn't come back. He was bullied at school for one terrifying year, after which he became a bully himself, began to smoke at the age of seven and to con money out of people by crying outside the post office and pretending he had no money for stamps to write home to his parents. A certain tendency to delinquency continued after he and his brother returned to England towards the end of the war and he attended Westminster School. His father was an aloof pathologist who cheated when playing chess with his son and was chronically unfaithful to his wife, as Simon discovered in adolescence, and as his mother confided in him a little later. It is tempting to apply Philip Larkin's well-known poem on mums and dads to Gray's case.

'During the period of my own adultery,' he reports, 'I frequently hovered on the verge of suicide – no, not suicide, something more violent, more of a sort of self-homicide – what I wanted really was to seize myself by the back of the neck and dash and dash my head, until my brains were out and I was over and done with.' He adds characteristically, 'On the other hand I didn't want to be dead.' After an extended affair with a colleague at Queen Mary College, Victoria Rothschild, he left Beryl, his wife of many years and the mother of his children, to marry Victoria. He was to the end of his life deeply in love with Victoria and deeply ashamed of his infidelity to Beryl, with no hope of resolving or reconciling these conflicting emotions. 'Through it all the moral toothache is throbbing away until it is all I really think about, why am I not a good man, why have I not done better, why am I sitting here chain-smoking in a rehearsal of my play . . .' This reference in *The Year of the Jouncer* is to *The Old Masters*, which Harold Pinter had generously agreed to direct in 2004 in spite of his own grave health problems, but the passage could come from anywhere in the later diaries, including – indeed especially – the last one, *Coda*, published posthumously in November 2008.

A coda is a concluding part of a musical or literary work that is additional rather than aesthetically essential, and Gray's *Coda* has this relation to the *Smoking Diaries* trilogy. The formal differences are relatively slight, but the tone and content are markedly more sombre. It begins with the writer taking two sleeping pills at 4 a.m. and promising himself that tomorrow he will write 'an account of what you've been told, on good medical authority, is the beginning of your dying'. But he fails. 'I keep sitting down to go on with this, again and again, night after night, but it's no good . . . one night I sat for a long time at my desk in my study without doing anything at all until I suddenly began to beat myself about the head.' It's not until he goes to Crete with Victoria for a two-week holiday in October 2007 that he is able to describe the bad news he received in July of that year and its sequel. A routine scan to check the state of a long-standing aneurysm revealed the presence of a tumour on a lung, soon followed by a tumour on his neck. Investigative surgery indicated that this was a secondary cancer and that the disease was spreading. The prognosis, which he didn't want to know, but which was pressed on him by an over-eager oncologist, was that he had a year to live – or nine months by the time he started to write about it.

Gray spares himself and his readers nothing in his account of the fear, depression, despair and self-reproach the knowledge of his condition generates, and the physical discomfort and personal indignities entailed in the medical consultations and investigations he undergoes. There are amusing anecdotes and sardonic observations, especially about the extraordinary insensitivity of the medics he encounters, but the humour is for the most part of the gallows variety, e.g. 'I've never needed cigarettes more than when getting the news that I'm dying from them.' In spite of that, he does cut down, and finds that the smell of other people's cigarette smoke disgusts him. The endless deferral of the last cigarette was a kind of running joke in the three preceding diaries, but Gray's plight now is no joke, and inevitably he broods on:

what in my nature made me a smoker? What in my nature allows me – sometimes it feels more like insistence – to go on smoking? The thought of dying terrifies me, the thought of dying of cancer particularly terrifies me, and yet – and yet – destiny is too grand a word, what I want is a word that has the meaning of a meeting up between the something in me that needs to smoke, call it a genetic disorder or call it original sin, and the something in me that needs the consequence, call it an effect, as in the law of cause and effect, or a punishment.

He concludes that he must have inherited a sense of sin from the Scots Presbyterians and Welsh Anglicans in his ancestry, but as a 'great-great-grandchild of the Enlightenment' he cannot seek absolution or justification from institutional religion. He records with admiration the courage and stoicism with which non-religious friends like the actor Alan Bates, Ian Hamilton and Harold Pinter,* faced the prospect of imminent death, but is unable to emulate them. All he can do is engage in painful self-examination, dramatised sometimes as a debate between two voices in his head, dubbed Thicko and Sicko, the first of whom jeers and accuses while the second wriggles uncomfortably and feebly defends himself. At times he sounds like one of Kierkegaard's angst-ridden personae, unable to embrace the Absurd of faith, but with no other relief – except writing itself.

There are moments of calm and evocations of simple available pleasures, especially the pleasure of swimming in the sea, which Gray describes in an earlier book as his 'favourite thing in life', and now as the way he

---

* Harold Pinter died on 24 December 2008, five months after Gray's death. His impressive fight against cancer, first diagnosed in 2002, and his determination to lead as full and as public a life as possible in spite of setbacks and complications, are reflected in many scenes and episodes of *The Smoking Diaries* trilogy.

would most like to leave it. 'I wish there were a way of just dissolving in the sea,' he writes, and finding himself overtired and out of his depth one day he would have let himself drown if it were not for the distress it would cause to Victoria. The book is dedicated to 'Victoria – without whom, nothing' and the tender but unsentimental way Gray records his dependence on her support is one of the elements that makes *Coda* a not unrelievedly harrowing book. There is a characteristic episode, both funny and poignant, where he worries about the large number of shoes, many unused, he possesses. Thinking she will find their disposal upsetting after his death he considers taking them secretly, pair by pair, to the Oxfam shop. 'But supposing she went into Oxfam, as she sometimes does, and saw all the shoes lined up against the wall there – what would she think? But why secretly? Surely I could say, "Darling, don't you think it's time –" No. Stop there.'

The Grays return to England to learn the result of the radiotherapy he received earlier. Setting off for the appointment with deep foreboding Gray resolves, 'Whatever it is . . . they will be my last words on the subject of myself.' To his stunned relief Dr Rootle (as Gray has prejudicially nicknamed him) reveals that the radiotherapy has been remarkably effective, and prognosticates possibly two years' remission. These are the last words of the book: 'I mean, two years, two whole – well eighteen months then, yes, let's keep it at eighteen months, in order to avoid disappointment.'

In the event Simon Gray lived for only nine more months, but felt relatively well during them, and what killed him – suddenly – was not the direct result of his drinking or smoking, but the rupture of the aneurysm, a fact which if, against his expectation, his spirit survives somewhere, will give him some ironic satisfaction. Whether by accident or inspired design there is a larger than normal number of blank pages – fifteen – at the back of the book, so as I approached the end, reading slowly to make the most of it, a diminishing but substantial wad of pages under my right thumb, I turned one and suddenly there were the last words – 'to avoid disappointment' – with only a few brief acknowledgements on the facing page and then a flutter of white leaves. Nothing could express more eloquently the abrupt removal of this writer from the world of the living, to the dismay of his friends and fans. But his brilliantly witty, searingly honest diaries will live on.

TERRY EAGLETON'S GOODBYE
TO ALL THAT

*A*FTER *THEORY*. BY Terry Eagleton. Anyone who served on the academic front of the culture wars in the closing decades of the twentieth century is likely to be arrested, or at least intrigued, by that conjunction of title and author.* For non-combatants a little contextual information may help to explain why. 'Theory' (usually printed with a capital T, and/or scare quotes, though not by Eagleton) is the loose and capacious term generally used to refer to the academic discourses which arose out of the impact of structuralism and post-structuralism on the humanities (or 'human sciences' as academics in Continental Europe, where it all started, prefer to call them). Key figures in its evolution were a brilliant generation of French intellectuals, including Roland Barthes, Jacques Lacan, Louis Althusser, Jacques Derrida and Michel Foucault, who turned upon the methodologies of the founding fathers of structuralism, such as the linguist Ferdinand de Saussure and the anthropologist Claude Lévi-Strauss, and the work of earlier seminal modern thinkers like Marx and Freud, a scrutiny that was at once critical and creative. To simplify

---

* Terry Eagleton, *After Theory* (London: Allen Lane, and New York: Basic Books, 2003).

drastically: structuralism offered to explain the meaning of all forms of cultural production by identifying the underlying systems of signification they employed, using the model of language; whereas post-structuralism argued that this pursuit of scientific objectivity is vain because culture is saturated in ideology and language itself provides no foundation for interpretative closure. One might say that Theory began when theory itself began to be theorised – or, in the buzz word of the day, 'deconstructed'.

In due course the movement's centre of gravity moved from France to America where it was developed and promulgated by writers like Paul de Man, J. Hillis Miller, Geoffrey Hartman, Jonathan Culler, Barbara Johnson, Gayatri Spivak, Fredric Jameson and Edward Said. In both continents it assimilated and theorised the nascent movement of feminist criticism. It extended the scope of traditional literary criticism to take in the whole range of cultural production, and it spawned a number of new, non-aesthetic approaches to this material under a bewildering variety of names – the New Historicism, post-colonial studies, subaltern studies, Queer Theory, and so on, each with its own jargon, periodicals and conferences. Most of these projects were seen, and saw themselves, as belonging to that even looser and larger phenomenon known as 'Postmodernism'. In this context the word is not merely descriptive of formal developments in the arts (as in 'post-modernist architecture' or 'the postmodernist novel'), but refers to family resemblances in a wide range of cultural attitudes and practices.

One very controversial effect of Theory on the academic study of literature was to undermine the authority of the traditional canon and to install in its place a set of alternative sub-canons such as women's writing, gay and lesbian writing, post-colonial writing, and the founding texts of Theory itself. It had its warmest welcome among smart young recruits to the academic profession, eager to try out this bright new methodological gadgetry with which they could dazzle and disconcert their elders. Not surprisingly Theory met with considerable resistance from those with a vested interest in more traditional modes of literary scholarship. There were many struggles over the curriculum, appointments, and tenure.

In England the most celebrated of these was the so-called MacCabe Affair of 1981 when a young lecturer at Cambridge University, Colin MacCabe, who had written a book about James Joyce much influenced by the new Parisian ideas, was denied the Cambridge equivalent of tenure. He and his supporters broadcast their belief that an injustice had been done, and the case seemed to tickle the fancy of the media, who had heard a lot about this newfangled structuralism without quite knowing what it was and were now able to discuss it in terms of personalities. What began as a row between members of the Cambridge English Faculty became a serial news story in the national and even international press, and culminated in a two-day debate in the University Senate where much academic dirty linen was washed in public. The traditionalists won inasmuch as Colin MacCabe was not given tenure (instead he became the youngest full professor of English in the UK at the University of Strathclyde) but it was a pyrrhic victory which led directly or indirectly to the departure of several of Cambridge's brightest stars, including Frank Kermode.

Eventually, and on a wider stage, Theory won, inasmuch as it had established itself by the early 1990s as a new orthodoxy in university humanities departments around the world, existing alongside the traditional practices of empirical historical scholarship and textual editing in a kind of uneasy détente, but definitely the dominant party in terms of influence, patronage, and prestige. The very success of Theory, however, eventually bred a kind of weariness in many of those who struggled on its behalf, and its institutionalisation deprived it of much of its original excitement and glamour. Disillusionment set in among some of its notable early supporters. Colin MacCabe, for instance, published a second edition of *James Joyce and the Revolution of the Word* in 2002 with an introduction that acknowledged the flaws in its theoretical apparatus, much of which, he said, 'has become a paralysing orthodoxy, trumpeted by dunces almost identical to those who freed me from my much loved Cambridge'. Sir Frank Kermode, whose staff/postgraduate seminar at University College London was an influential conduit for the ideas and personalities of Continental structuralism in the late 1960s and early 1970s, expressed increasing dismay in his later publications at the distorting effect of Theory on the appreciation and understanding of literature, especially the literature of the past. Frank Lentricchia, exponent of a Foucault-influenced, post-Marxist brand of political criticism in books like *Criticism and Social Change* (1983), published a confessional article in the magazine *Lingua Franca* in 1996 in which he denounced Theory for killing the pleasure of reading, deplored its effect on his indoctrinated graduate students, and revealed that he now taught Great Books rhapsodically to undergraduates behind closed doors. Examples could be multiplied of formerly committed partisans of Theory who have changed tack, diversified into creative writing and autobiography, re-dedicated themselves to teaching in encounter-group style, or left the academy altogether to become psychotherapists.

Terry Eagleton has a special place in the history of Theory, both in Britain and internationally. He was something of an *enfant terrible* as a tutor and lecturer at Cambridge in the early 1960s, where he obtained his BA and doctorate, and retained this aura after moving to Oxford where he eventually became Thomas Wharton Professor, characteristically attacking the previous occupant, John Bayley, in his inaugural lecture. Prince Charles once remarked to a group of Rhodes Scholars at Oxford that he hoped they were not taught by 'that dreadful Terry Eagleton', the only recorded comment on a literary critic by a member of the Royal Family. Eagleton revelled in shocking the academic establishment, and for a time the Roman Catholic establishment too. A working-class Catholic by birth and upbringing, he joined the Young Socialists while still at school, and as a student at Cambridge he was taught by Raymond Williams, the leading left-wing literary critic of his generation, with whom he had a somewhat Oedipal relationship for many years, being both indebted to and disapproving of different aspects of Williams's work. Through the Blackfriars communities in Cambridge and Oxford he also came under the spell of two politically and theologically radical Dominican friars, first Laurence Bright and later Herbert

McCabe (no relation to Colin). In the 1960s Eagleton was deeply involved in the production of a short-lived but lively left-wing Catholic periodical called *Slant* which identified the Kingdom of God with the Marxist ideal of a classless society, and condemned the then popular service of Benediction (in which a consecrated host is exposed and venerated to the accompaniment of prayers and hymns) as a liturgical perversion that turned the shared bread of the authentic Eucharist into a reified commodity.

Eagleton's first, precocious monograph, published in 1967, when Continental structuralism was little more than a rumour in English universities, was a conventional Marxist reading of Shakespeare's plays. In subsequent books like *Criticism and Ideology* and *Marxism and Literary Criticism*, both published in 1976, a time when structuralism was mutating into post-structuralism on the Continent, he engaged earnestly with the theoretical revision of Marxism being carried out by the French writers Louis Althusser and Pierre Macherey. Eagleton's leftist political principles made him suspicious of the formalist bias of structuralism, and more receptive to some aspects of post-structuralist Theory than to others – to post-colonial and feminist criticism rather than deconstruction, for instance. But his agile intelligence, eloquence and wit enabled him to grasp and expound the essential ideas of all of them in an accessible and even entertaining way. His *Literary Theory: An introduction* (1983) was a polemical as well as descriptive work, which proposed the replacement of literary studies by cultural studies, and came down heavily in its last chapter in favour of 'Political Criticism', but it covered the whole waterfront of Theory. It was seized and devoured with relief and gratitude by several generations of students, and is reported to have sold 800,000 copies world-wide – an astonishing figure and impressive testimony to Eagleton's global fame.

The title *After Theory*, therefore, inevitably provokes the question: is Terry Eagleton the latest of the stars of Theory to lose faith in it? The answer is: yes and no, or rather no and yes. *After Theory* is a kind of dialogue between Eagleton the Practitioner and Defender of Theory and Eagleton the Conscience and Accuser of Theory, or, one might say, between Terry the stand-up comedian and Terry the lay preacher. One of the difficulties of grappling with the book is that it is constantly using one voice to qualify the arguments of the other, but from about halfway onwards the second, more serious and critical voice dominates. On page one the author declares: 'Those to whom the title of this book suggests that "theory" is now over, and that we can all relievedly return to an age of pre-theoretical innocence, are in for a disappointment' – but so are those who hoped for a panegyric to the age of Theory.

It must be said that the quality of the writing is very uneven. Eagleton's racy, relaxed and humorous style of exposition is usually a refreshing change from the tortuous solemnity more typical of Theory, but in the first half of this book it sometimes seems merely slapdash. There are sentences that should never have got past the first draft on his computer screen, let alone into print, like: 'Much of the world as we know it, despite its solid, well-upholstered appearance, is of recent vintage.' (In the next sentence this upholstered vintage is thrown up by tidal waves.) There is a plethora of facetiously hyperbolic simile. This was always a favourite Eagleton trope, but it is in danger of becoming a distracting verbal tic, as, for instance, when postmodernism is criticised for attacking a bourgeois culture that is already on the wane: 'this is rather like firing off irascible letters to the press about the horse-riding Huns or marauding Carthaginians who have taken over the Home Counties.' It is not. The frequent use of *in any case, anyway, even so*, sometimes twice in the same paragraph, is another annoying stylistic feature. These words and phrases allow Eagleton to wriggle out of an apparent contradiction between two propositions by asserting something else at a higher level of generality. Thus in the first few pages he says, 'in a historic advance sexuality is now firmly established within academic life as one of the keystones of human culture'; then he says that most of this work is trivial and self-indulgent, and then: 'Even so, the advent of sexuality and popular culture as kosher subjects of study has put paid to one powerful myth . . . the puritan dogma that seriousness is one thing and pleasure another.' Perhaps this is dialectical thinking, but it often seems more like having it both ways.

He begins by locating the origins of Theory in the 1960s and that decade's heady ferment of liberation politics, youthful revolt and intellectual adventurousness. Bliss was it in that dawn to be alive . . . For a brief period it seemed possible that iconoclastic cultural criticism, avant-garde art and revolutionary politics might march confidently into the future arm in arm. But by the end of the 1970s the dream had faded, and in the greedy anti-ideological 1980s the left had to face the fact of its defeat. Eagleton observes astutely: 'As often happens, ideas had a last, brilliant efflorescence when the conditions which produced them were already disappearing. Cultural theory was cut loose from its moment of origin, yet tried in its way to keep that moment warm. Like war, it became the continuation of politics by other means.' That comment explains the ambivalence towards Theory which runs through the whole book. On the one hand Eagleton admires it for continuing to question the accepted 'order of things'; on the other he cannot forgive it for turning away from radical political action, which it regarded as 'fatally compromised by the emptiness of desire, the impossibility of truth, the fragility of the subject, the lie of progress, the pervasiveness of power'. Much of the blame for this *trahison des clercs* is attributed to the climate of postmodernism, which denies the validity of universals and first principles, and encourages a kind of hedonistic pick-'n'-mix browsing in the cultural shopping mall of ideas and experiences, depriving even ostensibly progressive projects, like post-colonial studies, of practical effect and moral purpose.

In a chapter called 'Losses and Gains' Eagleton attempts a kind of audit of Theory. He begins by taking a swing at the wilfully obscure and mystifying style of much of its literature, citing just one, unattributed sentence, evidently taken from some crazed deconstructionist intent on out-Derridaing Derrida:

> The in-choate in-fans ab-original para-subject cannot be theorized as functionally *completely* frozen in a world where teleology is schematised into geo-graphy.

It's a pity that Eagleton did not choose some longer, less extreme and more contextualised example of post-structuralist critical discourse – heaven knows there are plenty to choose from – analysing its rhetorical perversity and attempting to explain how and why this style of exposition became fashionable. His comment on this example is disappointingly weak:

> There is something particularly scandalous about *radical* cultural theory being so wilfully obscure . . . because the whole idea of cultural theory at root is a democratic one. In the bad old days, it was assumed that culture was something you needed to have in your blood, like malaria or red corpuscles. Countless generations of breeding went into the ways a gentleman could instantly distinguish a sprightly metaphor from a shopsoiled one. Culture was not something you could acquire, any more than you could acquire a second pair of eyebrows or learn to have an erection.

Reading this, one wonders exactly what bad old days Terry Eagleton is alluding to, only to discover incredulously that they went right up to the era of the Beatles:

> Theory, which we have seen was born somewhere in the dense, democratic jungle of the 1960s, thought otherwise. All you needed in order to join in the game was to learn certain ways of talking, not to have a couple of thoroughbreds tethered outside the door.

This is an absurd misrepresentation of the real history of literary criticism and literary education in the modern era. The teaching of vernacular literature in schools, colleges and universities was begun in the late nineteenth century and expanded in the twentieth precisely as a way of opening up 'culture' to all. And over the same period literary criticism evolved more and more sophisticated and illuminating 'ways of talking' about it. In England and America this project was furthered by what came to be called the New Criticism, extending roughly from the 1920s to the 1950s (or, say, I.A. Richards to W.K. Wimsatt) which contained a good deal of literary theory, even though it was not as systematic as the structuralist poetics and narratology developed over the same time-scale in Moscow, St Petersburg, Prague and in due course Paris. These two critical traditions remained curiously ignorant of each other until the 1960s. As Frank Kermode explained in his memoir *Not Entitled*, he and like-minded Anglo-American critics (among whom I would count myself) gave a warm welcome at first to European structuralism because they thought it might bring a new energy and rigour to a common pursuit.

Terry Eagleton knows all this of course, so why he should pretend otherwise is baffling. In the process the really important issue of the obfuscatory style of much Theory gets lost, or brushed aside. To demonstrate that it is not incompatible with the sensitive reading of literary texts he provides a little commentary on the opening sentence of a short story by Evelyn Waugh. This is perceptive enough but could have been done by any competent critic completely ignorant of the theory (i.e. Theory) which is the ostensible subject of his book. 'That theory is incapable of close reading is one of its opponents' most recurrent gripes,' he says. Is it? I would have said that a more common gripe against Theory is that its exponents are manically obsessive close readers whose interpretative ingenuity is unrestrained by traditional criteria of verifiability and plausibility. However, it is equally perverse to credit 'cultural theory' with demolishing the assumption 'that there is a single correct way to interpret a work of art'. 'Ambiguity' was a key term in the New Criticism, and William Empson's *Seven Types of Ambiguity* one of its seminal texts.

The chapter continues in this style, pitting caricatured 'conservative critics' against idealised 'cultural theorists' (I particularly cherish the phrase 'theory, in its unassuming way . . .') to reach the conclusion that 'most of the objections to theory are either false or fairly trifling'. At precisely this point, just about halfway through the book, when the informed reader may feel inclined to hurl it across the room in exasperation, Eagleton performs a stunning argumentative somersault:

> A far more devastating criticism of it can be launched. Cultural theory as we have it promises to grapple with some fundamental problems, but on the whole fails to deliver. It has been shamefaced about morality and metaphysics, embarrassed about love, biology, religion and revolution, largely silent about evil, reticent about death and suffering, dogmatic about essences, universals and foundations, and superficial about truth, objectivity and disinterestedness.

The rest of *After Theory* is an elaboration of this formidable indictment and an exposition of its philosophical basis.

First, Eagleton defends the idea that there is such a thing as 'absolute truth', using a homespun style of ordinary language philosophy. 'It simply means that if a statement is true, then the opposite of it can't be true at the same time, or true from some other point of view . . . it does not make sense to say there is a tiger in the bathroom from my point of view but not from yours.' Fair enough, but the next example is not so straightforward: '"Racism is an evil" is not the same kind of proposition as "I always find the smell of fresh newsprint blissful." It is more like the statement "There is a tiger in the bathroom."' More like, perhaps, but not the same. What constitutes racism is always open to interpretation and debate, whereas what constitutes a tiger is not. Deconstructionists will not feel seriously threatened by the argument so far.

Eagleton then moves on to 'the question of human well-being', which he seeks to define by a synthesis of Aristotle (whose *Ethics* he has obviously been studying carefully), Judeo-Christian moral teaching, and Marxism:

> Aristotle thought that there was a particular way of living which allowed us . . . to be at our best for the kind of creatures we are. This was the life conducted according to the virtues. The Judeo-Christian tradition considers that it is the life of charity or love. What this means . . . is that we become the occasion for each

other's self-realization. It is only through being
the means of your self-fulfilment that I can
attain my own . . . The political form of this
ethic is known as socialism, for which, as Marx
comments, the free development of each is the
condition for the free development of all.

There is no explicit acknowledgement that in political
and economic practice (e.g., in Russia and eastern Europe
under communism) 'socialism' on the Marxist model
proved inimical to people's free development, and was
decisively rejected by them when they had the opportunity,
but Eagleton does concede that 'it looks as though we
simply have to argue with each other about what self-
realization means; and it may be that the whole business
is too complicated for us to arrive at a satisfactory solution'.
At such times he sounds surprisingly like the pragmatists
and liberal humanists from whom he usually dissociates
himself. He criticises Marx for asserting that morality is
just ideology: '"moral" means exploring the texture and
quality of human behaviour as richly and sensitively as
you can . . . This is morality as, say, the novelist Henry
James understood it . . .' (And, one might add, as critics
like I.A. Richards and F.R. Leavis and Lionel Trilling
understood it.) It is not a matter, Eagleton finds, on
which Theory has had much that is useful to say. For
Derrida, for instance, 'ethics is a matter of absolute decisions – decisions which are vital and necessary, but also
"impossible", and which fall outside all given norms,
forms of knowledge and modes of conceptualization'.
Eagleton comments drily: 'One can only hope that he is
not on the jury when one's case comes up in court.'

The epigrams are sharper and smarter in this half of the book. E.g., 'Politics belonged to the boardroom, and morality to the bedroom. This led to a lot of immoral boardrooms and politically oppressive bedrooms' and 'Military technology creates death but destroys the experience of it'. Eagleton is especially interesting on the subject of death, and rises to a fine pitch of prophetic eloquence when denouncing both postmodernism and late capitalism for trying to deny its inevitability:

> The body, that inconvenient reminder of mortality, is plucked, pierced, etched, pummelled, pumped up, shrunk and remoulded. Flesh is converted into sign, staving off the moment when it will subside into the sheer pornographic meaninglessness of a corpse. Dead bodies are indecent: they proclaim with embarrassing candour the secret of all matter, that it has no obvious relation to meaning. The moment of death is the moment when meaning haemorrhages from us . . . Capitalism too, for all its crass materialism, is secretly allergic to matter . . . For all its love affair with matter, in the shape of Tuscan villas and double brandies, capitalist society harbours a secret hatred of the stuff. It is a culture shot through with fantasy, idealist to its core, powered by a disembodied will which dreams of pounding Nature to pieces.

'Death represents Nature's final victory over culture,' Eagleton declares, and thus also over Theory inasmuch as the latter asserts that everything is cultural.

★   ★   ★

The work of academic critics is seldom interpreted with reference to their biographies, but Terry Eagleton's critique of Theory owes much to his Roman Catholic background, vividly recalled in his highly entertaining memoir, *The Gatekeeper*. In Salford, the drab Lancashire industrial town where he grew up, there was, somewhat incongruously, an enclosed community of Carmelite nuns, to whom the young Eagleton acted as altar-server and 'gatekeeper' – passing them messages and objects via a turntable set into the convent wall, and ushering rare visitors into the forbidding parlour where they could communicate with the inmates through a grille. The nuns' life of total self-denial was by any secular criteria absurd, but it was a Kierkegaardian kind of absurdity that witnessed to the fallen state of the world, a world perceived as so sinful that the best thing to do was to withdraw from it, pray for it, and wait to be released from it. The young Terry Eagleton was impressed, but as he grew up and shed the simple faith instilled in him as a child, he replaced the concept of sin with the concept of political and economic oppression, and looked for salvation in this world rather than the next. 'One can move fairly freely . . . from Catholicism to Marxism without having to pass through liberalism,' he explains in *The Gatekeeper*. But he never completely severed the connection with his Catholic roots, partly because of those radical English Dominicans, especially Herbert McCabe whose influence on *After Theory* he acknowledges as all-pervasive.

McCabe (who died in 2001) was something of a maverick priest, even by the tolerant standards of the English Dominican province, and was once disciplined and sacked from the editorship of the order's journal, *New Blackfriars*, for declaring in an editorial that the Church was 'quite plainly corrupt'. (When reinstated years later he began his next editorial with the words, 'As I was saying when I was so oddly interrupted . . .') As a writer and preacher he tried to divest the Christian faith of 'religion', which had overlaid the essential message of the gospels – a message that had much in common with utopian socialism – with superstition, rules, and hierarchical authority. McCabe was adept at using modern biblical scholarship to defamiliarise the scriptures and surprise people into a perception of their radical nature, and traces of his teaching are visible in *After Theory*. By contrast with Derrida's inscrutable and ineffable ethical imperatives, Eagleton says, 'The New Testament's view of ethics is distinctly irreligious . . . What salvation comes down to [in Matthew's gospel] is the humdrum material business of feeding the hungry, clothing the naked and visiting the sick . . . The New Testament also adopts a fairly relaxed attitude to sex, and takes a notably dim view of the family.' (This last observation presumably refers to Jesus's friendly relations with fallen women, his exhortation to disciples to leave their families and follow him, and the snubbing of 'his mother and his brothers' in Luke 8.19–21.)

When you read McCabe you realise it was from him that Terry Eagleton learned to discuss complex abstract issues in accessible language and through homely analogies. For instance, in an essay on evil, the Dominican asserts that badness is just a particular lack of goodness, which doesn't mean it's not real: 'It would be absurd to say that holes in socks are unreal and illusory just because the hole isn't made of anything and is purely an absence.' McCabe maintained that 'when we speak of God we do not know what we are talking about. We are simply using language from the familiar context in which we understand it . . . to point . . . into the mystery that surrounds and sustains the world.' Presumably he believed in the reality of that ineffable ultimate transcendental signified, but Eagleton goes a step further, into what seems indistinguishable from atheism. 'God is the reason why there is anything at all rather than just nothing. But that is just another way of saying that there really isn't any reason.'

Nevertheless, the Christian counsels of perfection remain relevant for Eagleton even when deprived of their traditional metaphysical foundations. Since the only purpose of human life is to live as fully as possible, death will always seem arbitrary, but just because it is inevitable we must live in acceptance of it; and renouncing property, or being in principle willing to renounce it, as socialism in its purest form requires, is a way of preparing ourselves to give up bodily life.* According to Eagleton, the greedy consumerism of contemporary Western society, driven by global capitalism and celebrated by postmodernism in the arts and

---

* A hostile reviewer of *After Theory,* William Deresiewicz, complained that 'someone who owns three homes shouldn't be preaching self-sacrifice' (*The Nation,* 16 February 2004). Paul Vallely, however, pointed out later that there were practical reasons for this multiple ownership: one home is in Coleraine where Eagleton's wife teaches, another one is in Lancashire where Eagleton teaches, and their main home is halfway between the two in Dublin ('Terry Eagleton: Class Warrior', *Independent,* 13 October 2007).

the media, is in denial of this truth, and so is Theory,
especially in America:

> The body is a wildly popular topic in US cultural
> studies — but this is the plastic, remouldable,
> socially constructed body, not the piece of
> matter that sickens and dies. Because death is
> the absolute failure to which we all eventually
> come, it has not been the most favoured of topics
> for discussion in the United States. The US
> distributors of the British film *Four Weddings and
> a Funeral* fought hard, if unsuccessfully, to change
> the title.

There is a vein of anti-American sentiment running
through *After Theory* which has long been characteristic
of the British far left and was inflamed by the war in
Iraq. It is not the first book to suggest that Theory has
had its day or lost its way, but perhaps the first of its
kind to be written in the shadow of 9/11 and the alarming
global upheaval that followed, thus lending the argument
an apocalyptic tone at times. 'The End of History was
complacently promulgated from a United States which
looks increasingly in danger of ending it for real,' Eagleton
observes, alluding to the title of a much publicised book
by Francis Fukuyama published in 1992; and he concludes:
'With the launch of a new global narrative of capitalism,
along with the so-called war on terror, it may well be
that the style of thinking known as postmodernism is
now approaching an end.' Since the United States is of
pivotal importance in global politics, and the academic
institutions of the United States have been particularly

hospitable to Theory and postmodernism, a causal connection is implied between these phenomena. But the United States is pivotal because it won the cold war, and became an unopposed military superpower which unluckily fell into the control of an arrogant and reckless administration under George W. Bush. This can hardly be blamed on Theory, or postmodernism.

The other main factor in the current global crisis, the rise of religious fundamentalism, especially but not exclusively of the Islamic persuasion, is certainly within Theory's field of competence, but Eagleton claims that its scepticism about general principles has prevented it from saying anything very constructive on the subject. He argues that the objection to religious fundamentalists is not that they have principles, but that they have the wrong ones; that they base their principles on the foundation of a text or texts, 'which is the worst possible stuff for the purpose'; and that they 'are ready to destroy the whole of creation for the purity of an idea'. Human beings, he says, must learn to 'live ironically. To accept the unfoundedness of our own existence is among other things to live in the shadow of death . . . To accept death would be to live more abundantly.' Unfortunately fundamentalists are not very appreciative of irony, and are apt to apply that last dictum to life in the next world rather than this. Terry Eagleton has no real answer to the threat which that paradoxical figure, the suicide bomber, at once martyr and murderer, presents to civilised society. (But then, who has?)

After Theory is an ambitious and thought-provoking book as well as an exasperating one, but it overestimates the importance of Theory and its influence outside the academy, while avoiding a proper analysis of its history inside. Theory has, after all, been an almost exclusively academic pursuit, driven by professional as well as intellectual motivations. In a period when the university job-market became increasingly competitive it provided an array of impressive metalanguages with which academics in the humanities could win their spurs and demonstrate their professional mastery. But to anyone outside the arena – 'the educated general reader', for instance – the excruciating effort of construing this jargon-heavy discourse far exceeded the illumination likely to be gleaned from it, so they stopped reading it, and non-specialist media stopped reviewing it, which was bad both for academia and culture in general. Some of Theory's achievements are genuine and permanent additions to knowledge, or intellectual self-knowledge. Eagleton is quite right to assert that we can never go back to a state of pre-Theory innocence, believing in the transparency of language or the ideological neutrality of interpretation. At its best, as a method of critical reading (in Roland Barthes's *S/Z*, say), Theory performed at a second remove what literature does to life – defamiliarising the object of its attention, and making us see it and enjoy it afresh. But like all fashions it was bound to have a limited life of novelty and vitality, and we are now living through its decadence without any clear indication of what will supersede it. 'Theory' has, in short, become boringly predictable to many people who were once enthused by it, and that *After Theory* is most interesting when its focus is furthest from its nominal subject is evidence that Terry Eagleton has become bored by it too.

Postscript

In 2003, when *After Theory* was published, Terry Eagleton was John Edward Taylor Professor of Cultural Theory at Manchester University, having left Oxford two years earlier. In 2008 he departed from Manchester to become Distinguished Professor of English Literature at the University of Lancaster and has since held a number of visiting professorships in universities in Ireland, America and other parts of the world. He continued to publish prolifically in this period – some dozen books up till 2012, with more announced for publication. (He wrote amusingly about the Trollopian scale of his output in *The Gatekeeper*, 'Whereas other academics worry about not being productive enough, my embarrassment has always been the opposite. Instead of finding myself unable to write books, I find myself unable to stop, to the point where some people have wondered if I am actually a committee.')

In retrospect it is clear that *After Theory* marked not only Terry Eagleton's disillusionment with Theory, but also an interesting new turn in his own work. This may explain why the writing in the first half of that book was so far below his usual standard: he wanted to make his valediction to Theory as positive as possible to avoid giving encouragement to conservative cultural critics, but his heart wasn't in the task. None of the titles he published in the next ten years contains the word 'theory' except for a 25th-anniversary edition of *Literary Theory* issued by the University of Minnesota Press, while several others reflect the urge evident in the second half of *After Theory*, to discuss big cultural and philosophical issues in a religious perspective and theological language. His output in the last decade includes *Holy Terror* (2005), *The Meaning of Life* (2007), *Trouble with Strangers: A Study of Ethics* (2008), *Reason, Faith and Revolution: Reflections on the God Debate* (2009), and *On Evil* (2010). 'Why are the most unlikely people, including myself, suddenly talking about God?' he asked, in the fourth of those books. 'Who would have expected theology to rear its head once more in the technocratic twenty-first century . . . Why is it that my local bookshop has suddenly sprouted a section labelled "Atheism"?' The answer to the last question was, of course, the publication of several books attacking religious belief from the point of view of atheistic materialism, especially two bestsellers, *The God Delusion* (2006) by the biologist and popular science writer Richard Dawkins, and *God is Not Great* (2007) by the American-based British journalist and author Christopher Hitchens. But those and similar books were themselves a response to the rise of militant Islamic fundamentalism, unforgettably manifested in the destruction of the Twin Towers in New York in September 2001, and its hostile counterpart, Christian fundamentalism (especially of the American variety), both of which were seen by liberal intellectuals as serious threats to the values of secular Western society.

Eagleton plunged into this arena of debate. In *Holy Terror* (2005) he tackled the subject of terrorism, tracing the phenomenon back through its first political manifestation in the French Revolution to its roots in ancient religion – the idea of martyrdom, the figure of the scapegoat, the Dionysian revolt against reason – drawing on literary texts from Euripides' *The Bacchae* to Conrad's *The Secret Agent,* 'the first suicide-bomber novel of English Literature'. He distinguishes neatly between the two aspects of that paradoxical figure. The martyr's death 'signifies a hope for the future, bearing witness to a truth and justice beyond the present. But whereas the martyr is prepared to stake his life on this, the suicide bomber is prepared to stake *your* life on it.' This makes it a genuinely evil act according to Eagleton's ethics. Unfortunately, 'the more Western society reacts to terrorist assault with answerable illegality, the more it depletes the very spiritual and political resources which it takes itself to be protecting . . . we . . . see . . . a similar inversion of victory and defeat in the case of the terrorists'. It's a plausible but depressing analysis, though the book as a whole is a stimulating tour de force.

In October 2006 Eagleton published a long review of *The God Delusion* in the *London Review of Books* which famously began: 'Imagine someone holding forth on biology whose only knowledge of the subject is the *British Book of Birds*, and you have a rough idea of what it feels like to read Richard Dawkins on theology.' Much of the review, which provoked a long-running correspondence in the *LRB*, was incorporated later in *Reason, Faith and Revolution*, where he also took on Christopher Hitchens, referring occasionally to the two authors under the compound name of 'Ditchens'. Eagleton is a witty and acute polemicist, and scored some effective points against the dogmatic atheism of his antagonists, but the

coherence of his own argument is debatable, especially
when expounded at book-length. He claims to be defending
'faith', not 'belief', against atheism.

> Faith, Ditchens seems not to register, is not
> primarily a belief that something or someone
> exists, but a commitment and allegiance – faith
> which might make a difference to the frightful
> situation you find yourself in, as is the case, say,
> with faith in feminism or anti-colonialism.
> Christian faith, as I understand it, is not primarily
> a matter of signing on for the proposition that
> there exists a Supreme Being, but the kind of
> commitment made manifest by a human being
> at the end of his tether, foundering in darkness,
> pain and bewilderment, who nevertheless
> remains faithful to the promise of a transforma-
> tive love.

There's a loophole in that 'primarily' which allows for
a more credal kind of faith, but few practising Christians,
and very few Catholics, I suspect, would define their
faith in these starkly existentialist terms. It seems more
like the Protestant concept of 'conversion', transposed
into a secular and politicised key. It evidently serves
Terry Eagleton well as something to live by, but it
provides a very fragile platform from which to argue
against the opponents of religion. While jeering sarcastic-
ally at the theological and biblical illiteracy of Ditchens,
he frequently expresses complete agreement with their
criticisms of Christian beliefs and practices, and becomes
almost fulsomely admiring at times (e.g.: 'Dawkins . . .

has done a magnificent job over the years of speaking out against that particular strain of psychopathology known as fundamentalism'). He makes it clear that he has no faith in the institutional Roman Catholic Church, in either its officially promulgated doctrines or its governance, though he respects individual members. Herbert McCabe remains a source of inspiration, and Eagleton frequently invokes his summary of the meaning of the crucifixion, 'If you don't love you're dead, and if you do, they'll kill you.'

> The Christian faith holds that those who are able to look on the crucifixion and live, to accept that the truth of human history is a tortured body, might just have a chance of new life – but only by virtue of an unimaginable transformation in our currently dire condition. This is known as the resurrection . . .

Shortly after expounding this idiosyncratic version of Christian faith Eagleton surprisingly concedes: 'It may well be that all this is no more plausible than the tooth fairy. Most reasoning people these days will see excellent grounds to reject it. But critics of the richest, most enduring form of popular culture in human history have a moral obligation to confront that case at its most persuasive.' Persuasive or not, as put by Eagleton it represents a very small fraction of the spectrum of Christian belief, and seems more appropriately described as the faith of a 'tragic humanist', which is how Eagleton defines himself at the end of *Reason, Faith and Revolution*. There is a paradox here: one of the weaknesses of

Dawkins's position is that he doesn't seem to acknowledge that his contentment with a universe that is ultimately purposeless and indifferent to human beings is fairly easy to achieve when you are privileged to live a comfortable and fulfilling life. Terry Eagleton does well to remind him and others of his persuasion that the lives of a large proportion of the human race are made chronically wretched by poverty, ill-health and violent oppression (and, one might add, just bad luck). For many of them religion is often the only thing that makes life meaningful and worth living, by its promise of a better life to come for those who deserve it. Materialistic atheism takes away that hope, which is rooted in a deep human desire for justice, but 'tragic humanism' – religion from which the supernatural has been stripped away – seems to do the same.

In *The Meaning of Life: A very short introduction*, Eagleton presented a more genial response to the enigmas of our existence. Its very title, on the cover of a little book measuring 11 cm x 17 cm and containing only a hundred pages, raises a smile, and the author shows he is well aware of its presumptuousness, while nevertheless managing to cover an enormous amount of philosophical ground in a lucid, pithy and entertaining way, with deftly chosen illustrations from world literature. It is a brilliant feat, which perhaps only Terry Eagleton could have pulled off. He is 'widely regarded as the United Kingdom's most influential living literary critic', according to Wikipedia, which cites four published sources to support this claim. He is probably the most well-known, and perhaps the most widely read – but is he the most influential? If there is a school of Eagletonian critics, I am not aware of it, and it is difficult to imagine that there could be. The man writes so much on such various topics, and changes the focus of his attention so often, that it would be impossible to derive a systematic critical method from his writings. His *métier* is to excite, provoke and stimulate our interest in literature and ideas by the breadth of his reading, the acuteness of his intelligence, and the energy of his prose. The style is the man, or rather the critic, and could not be imitated without turning into pastiche or parody. It is comparable to the style of a first-class journalist – and I mean that as a compliment – applied to information of great intellectual complexity and breadth of historical reference such as is usually encountered only in works of specialist scholar-ship, making it accessible, comprehensible, and enter-taining as well as instructive.

FRANK REMEMBERED — BY A
KERMODIAN

THE NAME OF Frank Kermode first impinged on my
consciousness in 1954, when I was a second-year
undergraduate reading English at University College
London. In our Shakespeare course we had lectures from
Winifred Nowottny, who in due course would be a
colleague of Frank's when he occupied the Lord North-
cliffe chair at UCL. Sadly, Winifred became increasingly
eccentric and obsessive towards the end of her life, but
in the early 1950s she was a charismatic teacher who
gave the impression that she was sharing with us her
own latest thoughts and discoveries about English literature, and we hung on her every word. Winifred read
Frank's New Arden edition of *The Tempest* when it first
came out and was greatly excited by its introduction, the
gist of which – the way, for instance, Shakespeare poetic-
ally explored contemporary concerns with the discovery
and colonisation of the New World – she expounded
with the book open in her hand. This, we inferred, was
the cutting edge of modern literary scholarship – and
we were not misled.

In 1960 I was appointed Assistant Lecturer in the
English Department of Birmingham University, and in
the Easter vacation of 1961 I attended what was then

called the University Teachers of English Annual Conference, held that year in Cambridge. Among the principal
speakers, along with W.K. Wimsatt and John Holloway,
was Frank Kermode, then occupying his first professorial
chair at Manchester. At this same conference I met Bernard
Bergonzi, whom Frank had appointed to an assistant
lectureship at Manchester. He had recently read my first
novel, *The Picturegoers*, and recognised the location of the
story as that of his own corner of south-east London, so
we became, and have remained, good friends. It was
probably through Bernard that I was introduced to Frank
at that conference, and was privileged to sit in someone's
bedroom drinking whisky with him and his companions
late one night. I was, as most people were, charmed by
his affable manners and quick wit, but I regret to say that
the only specific topic of his conversation that I recall
concerned the performance of his new Mini on the drive
down from Manchester. The Mini was then, however, a
novel and trendy vehicle, and seemed an appropriate
possession for a cutting-edge scholar.

My subsequent acquaintance with Frank was for
several years maintained principally through meetings at
other conferences and similar academic occasions, but it
eventually became a valued personal friendship. In the
meantime he became for me, as for many others, an
inspirational literary critic through his books, articles and
reviews. I still remember the grateful wonder with which
I read *The Sense of an Ending* (1967), a book of modest
length but breathtaking scope. For me it was a seminal
work which had the effect of extending my critical
interest in the novel from a preoccupation with verbal
style (exemplified in my first book of criticism, *Language*

of Fiction) to an engagement with broader questions of narrative structure – for example, peripeteia, the technical term for a sudden reversal of circumstances and expectations in a plot, which Kermode compared to the constantly revised predictions of the end of the world in the history of Christianity.

> Peripeteia, which has been called the equivalent, in narrative, of irony in rhetoric, is present in every story of the least structural sophistication. Now peripeteia depends on our confidence of the end; it is a disconfirmation followed by a consonance; the interest of having our expectations falsified is obviously related to our wish to reach the discovery or recognition by an unexpected and instructive route . . . So that in assimilating the peripeteia we are enacting that readjustment of expectation in regard to an end which is so notable a feature of naive apocalyptic. And . . . we are . . . reenacting the familiar dialogue between credulity and scepticism. The more daring the peripeteia, the more we may feel that the work respects our sense of reality.

The point may seem obvious enough today, but to me in 1967 it seemed like a revelation, the elegant lucidity of the exposition making it all the more persuasive. *The Sense of an Ending* was full of such illuminations. It made me receptive to the new structuralist narratology which was to come out of Europe, and especially France, in the next decade, and which Frank himself did much to interpret and disseminate in his writings (in a more reader-friendly style than that of the Parisian *savants*) and through a famous graduate seminar, hospitable to visitors, which he ran at UCL in the late 1960s and early 1970s.

The concept of 'apocalypse', the prophetic revelation of an end, which runs like a thread through *The Sense of an Ending* proved a useful key to the understanding of much modern literature, notably D.H. Lawrence (whom Frank radically and convincingly reinterpreted), and also of postmodernism. His essay 'Objects, Jokes and Art' which first appeared in *Encounter* in its heyday (1966) is a brilliant, witty and elegant analysis of aleatory art, literature and music, such as Duchamp's 'ready-made' sculptures, William Burroughs's *Nova Express*, composed of cut-up fragments of printed texts, and John Cage's silent piano piece 4' 33", which focuses the auditors' attention on random sounds in the environment for the prescribed number of minutes and seconds. I selected this essay as the last item in my Reader, *20th Century Literary Criticism* (1972), and it was pleasing to conclude an anthology of nearly 700 pages with Frank's final sentence: 'In the end what Simone Weil called "decreation" (easy to confuse with destruction) is the true modernist process in respect of form and the past. Or if it is not we really shall destroy ourselves at some farcical apocalypse.'

His interest in the idea of apocalypse later led Frank into the area of biblical criticism and textual scholarship, and once again I found myself learning from him – this time about texts that were almost boringly familiar from my Roman Catholic background. *The Genesis of Secrecy* (1979) defamiliarised the gospels. Reviewing that book in the *New Statesman*, I commented:

He himself writes as a declared 'secular' critic, yet in the end he seems more dejected than are most Christians by the discovery that the truth about the historical Jesus is irrecoverable, not (to borrow a metaphor from Conrad) inside the gospels like a kernel, but 'outside, enveloping the tale which brought it out only as a glow brings out a haze.' Kermode accepts the infinite plurality of interpretation whatever kind of text is in question, but for him this acceptance is tragic, since we interpret over and over again in quest of a truth that we know is unobtainable. 'World and book, it may be, are hopelessly plural, endlessly disappointing,' he elegiacally concludes. *The Genesis of Secrecy*, however, does not disappoint. It is exactly what one expects from Professor Kermode: elegant, incisive, expert, and original. What could not have been predicted is that it would make the New Testament as interesting to the literary critic as Joyce or Kafka.

From Frank's urbane, relaxed manner and fluent, educated speech you would never have guessed that he was brought up in a poor family and underprivileged environment on the Isle of Man. I remember him telling me ruefully once that his friends in America (where he was always much in demand as a visiting professor and celebrity lecturer) could never understand why he had such poor-looking teeth, being quite unable to conceive the lack of dental care and hygiene in British working-class society between the wars. But it was not until I read his memoir *Not Entitled* in 1995 that I fully comprehended the disadvantages in early life which he had overcome to make his brilliant career. His father was a storeman, his mother a farm girl and later a waitress. The family lived first in a tenement and then in a council house 'designed by somebody who had a very low opinion of the needs and deserts of the lower classes'.

The young Kermode had his Wordsworthian moments – notably an epiphany experienced while on an errand one autumn evening, between the ironmonger's shop and the Congregational chapel. 'The faint smudged pink of the sky above the church complied with the noises of the street and the tread of unilluminated persons, who had no notion of the plenitude of which they were part.' Elated by this sudden apprehension of the wonder of creation and his own place in it, the boy put a question to God: 'Did other persons, when they ate oranges, experience the taste I had of orange?' No answer was forthcoming, but merely to pose it was evidence of an unusually enquiring mind, precociously identifying the problematic nature of what cognitive scientists and philosophers of mind call 'qualia', and still find puzzling.

Precocity can, however, be a liability. Kermode won his scholarship to high school a year earlier than usual and was therefore always by far the youngest boy in his class. Fat, bespectacled, and without physical grace or dexterity (his father called him a *phynodderee,* the charming Manx word for a clumsy fairy), he was unmercifully bullied at school and soon lost the will or ability to learn. Ashamed to let his parents see how badly he had performed, he falsified a school report – a traumatic episode which he still found painful to recall in his memoir. The boy, in short, was deeply unhappy, and suffered something like a nervous breakdown. He recovered in time to win another scholarship, to Liverpool University, but the misery of those pubescent years sowed the seeds of anxiety and self-doubt in later life. Even at the height of his professional fame Frank Kermode always felt himself to be an outsider, almost an imposter. 'Looking the part while not being quite equal to it seems to be something I do rather well.'

What most impressed me in the memoir was its vivid account of his service in the Royal Navy during the Second World War, which alternated periods of extreme tedium and discomfort with moments of lethal danger. Entitled 'My Mad Captains', alluding to a series of variously deranged superior officers under whom he served, this section of the book is as funny and alarming as anything in Evelyn Waugh's *Sword of Honour.* Kermode, who had worked on the Liverpool–Isle of Man steamers as a student in his vacations, volunteered for the navy, and became, in due course, a lieutenant. His first ship was the *Sierra*, a slow, unlovely merchantman hastily converted for naval duties, commanded by Captain Stonegate, a decorated but traumatised survivor of Dunkirk, whom Kermode first encountered threatening indolent dockside workers with a revolver. Kermode reported to a Lieutenant Taylor, a gloomy pale-faced man who lived on an exclusive diet of pink gin and canned lambs' tongues and who died two days later, possibly as a consequence of it. Kermode stepped into his shoes as Stonegate's secretary, but before long the deranged captain blew his brains out with his revolver. His successor, Henty, fell down a staircase and broke both legs before Kermode could ascertain whether he was mad. The next captain, Archer, certainly was: a monster of the kind it is amusing to read about, but hell to live with. Gross of physique and appetite, cunning, venal and utterly dedicated to the furtherance of his own interest, he enjoyed humiliating his subordinates, and never bothered even to learn the name of his lieutenant, addressing him indifferently as Cosmo, Cosmos and Comody. Under his command the crew of the *Sierra* laboured vainly to lay anti-submarine booms outside the Icelandic harbour of Reykjavic for nearly two years of excruciating boredom, vile weather, physical discomfort and sexual deprivation. Once, in his cups, Archer set off on a suicidal voyage into the teeth of a force 10 gale in sub-zero temperature. 'He poured himself a Scotch. "Well, Comody," he said, "it seems we've fucking 'ad it."' Frank Kermode certainly thought so, but somehow the old tub survived.

Under a new captain, not mad for once, but a rather unpleasant martinet, the *Sierra* sailed to the Mediterranean as part of a convoy supplying the Allied forces in North Africa, and on this voyage Kermode first experienced enemy action. He was in a lavatory at the time, and arrived on deck a little late, to see two British ships on fire, presumably torpedoed, and destroyers scattering depth charges as a solitary Catalina circled the convoy. After an interval the survivors in a lifeboat rowing away from one of the burning ships inexplicably returned to board it, and almost immediately the ship exploded, blowing them to smithereens. The Catalina now proceeded, in breach of strict regulations, to fly along the line of the convoy, and since it was known that the Germans were using captured Catalinas, it was promptly shot down with the loss of all its crew, who proved in due course to be Canadian. Kermode laconically comments: 'It is interesting to note that none of the people who died in this little action need have done so.' He ended the war in the Pacific as a member of the crew of an aircraft carrier who expected, with some trepidation, to take part in the final assault on Japan. They were spared this ordeal by the dropping of the atomic bomb on Hiroshima. 'The general opinion was that it saved our lives, and we were unethically pleased about this' – a reaction which I find entirely forgivable.

That chapter of *Not Entitled* is so good that you wonder with regret why Frank decided after he was demobilised that his ambitions to be a creative writer were doomed and abandoned them to become an academic. Perhaps the two vocations seemed less compatible then than they did to my generation. I was born in 1935, just old enough to remember what it was like to live through the Second World War as a civilian, and to acquire from comic books and movies a rather simplified and heroic idea of what it was like for combatants; later I was a reluctant conscript, doing boring and banal National Service in the peacetime army. As a young university teacher I was often struck by the thought that many of my distinguished senior colleagues in the field of English Literature had seen active service in the war, yet very seldom spoke about it, and almost never referred to it in their published work. Would one have guessed, without being told,

that, for example, Raymond Williams had commanded
a tank in Normandy, Richard Hoggart slogged through
North Africa and Italy with the artillery, Philip Brock-
bank piloted bombers over Germany, and Graham
Hough and Ian Watt were prisoners of war in the
notorious Japanese camps of Siam? I thought not; yet
surely to have been in such life-threatening situations
would leave its mark on a man, and make him take a
somewhat different view of, say, cruces in Shakespeare's
texts, or symbolism in D.H. Lawrence, or the Intentional
Fallacy, from those who had not had such experience?
Not so, according to Kermode. The experience of modern
warfare is so absurd, so chaotic and random, that there
is really nothing to be learned from it except that it is
better to be lucky than to be unlucky – and even that
is not an unmixed blessing. Frank counted himself fortunate, but nourished a vague sense of guilt, common
among survivors of war, who 'have somewhere in their
heads the notion that they have remained alive by some
slightly underhand trick or evasion'. As he observes, one
might expect that those who for one reason or another
had had a safe, cushy war, or avoided it altogether, would
be the ones troubled by guilt and low self-esteem: 'But
it doesn't work like that, it never did.' This helps to
explain why in spite of being by his own admission a
workaholic driven by academic ambition, at some cost
to his personal relationships and family life, a man who
occupied some of the most prestigious professorial chairs
of English Literature in Britain and was knighted in 1991,
his social manner was always modest, unassertive and
ironically self-deprecating.

In an interview once Frank said, rather sadly, apropos

of the flamboyant Yale professor Harold Bloom, that 'there aren't any Kermodians in the world', meaning that he himself hadn't attracted disciples like Bloom (or, one might add, like F.R. Leavis, Raymond Williams, Northrop Frye and Jacques Derrida). This is true in the sense that Frank never formulated a critical 'method' or ideological apparatus which could be simply appropriated and applied by others. But many of us who pursued academic careers in what looks in retrospect like the Golden Age of English studies (from, say, the mid-1950s to the mid-1980s) were covert Kermodians inasmuch as we regarded him as the most accomplished literary critic of his generation. Firstly, he wrote beautifully – a graceful, precise, apparently effortless prose. If its vocabulary is occasionally challenging, that is because of his unusual range and elegant economy of reference, not because of any professional pomposity or deliberate mystification. He was a master of the review-essay of the kind he published frequently in the *New York Review of Books* and the *London Review of Books*, where in a few thousand words he would spin original thoughts of his own on a variety of topics out of a courteous but searching encounter with another mind. He wrote in a late collection of such essays that criticism 'can be quite humbly and sometimes even magnificently useful', but it must 'also give pleasure'. It was the anhedonist character of much post-structuralist discourse as much as its theoretical principles that made Frank turn against it in his later years, and led him to say that it had had an 'interestingly catastrophic' effect on literary studies. Secondly (and this is one reason why there are no card-carrying Kermodians) he was enormously wide-ranging and indefatigably

curious in his intellectual interests. Renaissance literature, Romanticism, symbolism, modernism, narratology,
hermeneutics and biblical criticism . . . Shakespeare,
Yeats, Lawrence, E.M. Forster, Henry Green, Muriel
Spark . . . The catalogue of authors and topics he wrote
about seems endless. Few modern academic critics ranged
so widely and to such effect. Thirdly, he never tried to
say the last word about any of the many topics he touched
upon. He was suggestive rather than exhaustive. He
passed you the ball and left you some space to run with
it yourself, and perhaps even score. That is possibly the
most cherishable attribute a critic can have.

Frank Kermode died in August 2010, at the age of ninety,
intellectually active to the last. I remember him with
great affection for his geniality, his self-deprecating
humour, his capacity to surprise you with an acute
observation, and to make you want to revise a lazy
thought or a careless expression. There was always, I
felt, an underlying melancholy in his temperament, but
a complete absence of self-pity. When I heard that he
was seriously ill and wrote to commiserate, he replied
characteristically: 'The news is, alas, true. When I read
Eothen for school cert I learned that in Kinglake's time
nobody any longer said "Alas!" but sometimes it does
duty if only as a sigh. I've done and allowed to be done
all that can be done and my friends come from the pain
controllers, not the oncologists. I'm grateful for others,
such as yourself, who have given me friendship and
pleasure.' In their unforced eloquence those words are
deeply expressive of the man who wrote them.

MALCOLM BRADBURY: WRITER
AND FRIEND

IN 1961, AGED twenty-six, I was in my second year as
Assistant Lecturer in English Literature at Birmingham
University when the Head of Department, Professor
Terence Spencer, decided that we ought to have a
specialist in American Literature, and accordingly adver-
tised a post for one. I remember being in his office one
day when he showed me an application for this lectureship from a man two years older than me called Malcolm
Bradbury, currently an extra-mural studies tutor at Hull
University. He was completing a PhD dissertation on
American literary expatriates and had a number of interestingly varied publications to his name, including a novel,
Eating People Is Wrong, which I had heard of, though not
read. 'I don't think we need bother interviewing anybody
else, do you?' Spencer said nonchalantly (heads of departments enjoyed the power of feudal barons in those days)
and I readily agreed. I was the only teacher in the department under thirty-five; I looked forward to having a
colleague of the same generation as myself, and one who
seemed to have the same ambition to combine an
academic career with writing fiction (at a time when
creative writing was not on the curriculum of any British
university). I had published my first novel in 1960, and

Malcolm his in 1959. Naturally I read *Eating People Is Wrong*, and naturally he read *The Picturegoers*, before he arrived in Birmingham in January 1962. We quickly became friends, as did our wives Mary and Elizabeth.

Malcolm was not quite my first 'writer-friend', but he was the one most important to me, and remained so until his death in the year 2000, at the age of sixty-nine. It left a space in my life that could never be filled. Our careers were so closely entwined, especially in the early years, that without that relationship my own would have been significantly different – much less interesting and possibly less successful. We soon found we had much in common, but it was more than I realised until I read the fragments of autobiography in *Liar's Landscape*, a posthumously published collection of miscellaneous writings edited by his son Dominic. We were both children of the war and the Blitz, traumatically separated for a time from home and parents, dimly aware of a vast historical drama being played out in which our little lives had been caught up with unpredictable consequences. It made both of us, I think, temperamentally cautious and prone to anxiety in later life, but ready to seize the opportunities which opened up in peacetime for the first beneficiaries of the 1944 Education Act. We both came from lower-middle-class backgrounds where there was no tradition of proceeding to higher education. My parents had to be convinced by the headmaster of my Roman Catholic grammar school that it would be a good idea for me to go to university, rather than to leave at sixteen and start earning my living. I literally didn't know there were other universities than Oxford, Cambridge and London and didn't for a moment consider applying to the first two, so I went to University College London to do (we didn't say 'read') English for my BA degree, commuting from home. Malcolm was encouraged by his grammar school to apply for Oxbridge, but because his father would not countenance his staying on in the sixth form for that purpose after taking 'A' Levels, he went to what was then the University College of Leicester. Since its students sat the London University External exams in those days, we pursued essentially the same syllabus in English, and later both of us obtained London MAs – then a two-year research degree – doing our research in the Round Reading Room of the British Museum, though in different years.

It is interesting to speculate what difference it would have made to our subsequent careers if we had gone to Oxbridge. I suspect Malcolm would have adapted to it better than I, and he might have stayed on to become a don. In later life he enjoyed being a visiting Fellow at Oxford, and for many summers chaired an annual seminar for foreign academics and writers run by the British Council in a Cambridge college. He always seemed very happy and at home in these settings – the smooth lawns, gravelled paths and ancient buildings soothed his spirit, and the ritual of hall and high table appealed to him – but the redbrick University College Leicester, housed in a converted lunatic asylum, a brief glimpse of which inspired Kingsley Amis to write *Lucky Jim*, provided more useful material for a first novel in the 1950s.

Although we had much in common, there were also important differences between us, more obvious in some of our books than others. I was a Londoner by birth and upbringing; Malcolm's roots, in spite of some early years in Metroland, were essentially provincial. He was born in Sheffield, grew up in Nottingham, and never felt at ease in the capital. In time he developed a liking for country life. When we met I was a practising and fairly orthodox Catholic, and several of my novels are concerned with Catholic hang-ups about sex and the loss of traditional faith. Malcolm enjoyed visiting empty village churches in the spirit of Philip Larkin's poem 'Church Going', but had no religious belief. He cherished the values of secular liberal humanism, and his novels are often about liberal humanists who lack the strength to resist forces in society that are inimical to those values. If our 'campus novels' were sometimes confused in the memories of readers, and we were occasionally congratulated on writing each other's books (a mistake difficult to correct graciously), that was partly because we drew on the same kind of experience, and found that we perceived the academic world with a similar sense of humour. Edith Wharton, writing in her memoirs about her friendship with Henry James, says, 'The real marriage of true minds is for any two people to possess a sense of humour or irony pitched in exactly the same key, so that their joint glances at any subject cross like inter-arching search-lights.' I often had that experience with Malcolm, long after he left Birmingham, when we heard in some senior common room or conference bar a remark or anecdote ripe with fictional possibilities, and our eyes would meet as if silently to say, 'Toss you for it?' But it was his influence and example that first encouraged me to develop an element of comedy which was present but subdued in my first two novels. I remember that in our very first conversation, he commented favourably on a parody in *The Picturegoers* of the bizarre names often listed in Hollywood film credits – a passage which I had regarded as an insignificant detail. Sometimes a remark like that from a source you respect can make you see your own work in an entirely new light.

Malcolm was already firmly established in the literary world when he arrived in Birmingham. *Eating People Is Wrong* had caused more of a stir than *The Picturegoers*, and he was a regular contributor to newspapers and magazines on a cultural spectrum that ran from *Punch* to the *Critical Quarterly*. His confident professionalism and readiness to turn his hand to any literary task, moving effortlessly from one stylistic register to another, impressed me and inspired emulation. I placed a few sketches in *Punch* myself, and in 1963 collaborated with Malcolm and a talented undergraduate in the Birmingham English Department, Jim Duckett, to write a satirical revue which would never have come into existence without Malcolm's initiative. Jim Duckett, whom I had tutored in his first year, wrote, produced and performed in a student revue in his second year which impressed Malcolm and me. Malcolm invited John Harrison, the Artistic Director of the Birmingham Rep, whom he had known in Nottingham, to see it, and persuaded him to commission a revue from the three of us for the Rep's autumn season. I have happy memories of hilarious script-writing sessions, Jim and I improvising as we paced up and down in Malcolm's office while he pounded out our lines on an upright typewriter, improving them in the process. We finished off the script in the summer vacation at the rented cottage near Beverley in East Yorkshire which

Malcolm and Elizabeth had retained after he left his job at Hull. The show, entitled *Between These Four Walls*, was a mixture of sketches and songs, inspired by *Beyond the Fringe* and the BBC's TV programme *That Was The Week That Was*. It was generally well received, though box office takings never recovered from the assassination of President Kennedy halfway through its four-week run. We writers each received £40 for our contributions. It was not a negligible sum at that date, but the fascinating and instructive experience of sitting in a theatre and registering every nuance of an audience's reaction to one's words was far more valuable. I discovered in myself a zest for satirical, parodic and farcical writing which found its expression in my next novel, *The British Museum is Falling Down*, dedicated 'To Malcolm Bradbury, whose fault it mostly is that I have tried to write a comic novel'. It was his favourite among my books.

Malcolm was always a great collaborator, and wrote an amusing account of his early enthusiasm for that form of literary composition, which was included in *Liar's Landscape*. I do not know whether it was literally true that he and his friend Barry Spacks, whom he met at the University of Indiana on his first visit to America in 1955–6, would bash away simultaneously at their typewriters until one called out 'Blocked!' and then change places and continue each other's stories, but it is a wonderful image, both sublime and ridiculous, of collaboration overcoming the frustrations and anxieties of the creative process.

Malcolm responded to the stimulus of other people's

ideas and could often see in them possibilities of which their originators were unaware, as I discovered shortly after he came to Birmingham. I had found in a local second-hand book shop a copy of a light romantic novel, by a completely forgotten novelist, published in 1915, called *Nymphet*. That is the familiar name given by the hero of the story to an eleven-year-old girl who facilitates his eventual union with his beloved. It is also of course the generic term applied by Humbert Humbert to the eponymous heroine of Vladimir Nabokov's celebrated novel, *Lolita*, published forty years later, generally assumed to be the first use of this archaic word in modern fiction. It was possible, by close reading and interpretative ingenuity, to see beneath the innocent sentimental surface of *Nymphet* the unconscious representation of an adult man's erotic attraction to a pre-pubescent girl, and to regard it therefore as some kind of precursor of Nabokov's masterpiece. It seemed to be an idea worth writing up, and I accordingly did so, and sent my essay to a few magazines – without success. I showed it to Malcolm and he offered to rewrite it and split the fee if he placed it. Being hard up at the time, I agreed. Malcolm transformed my straightforward essay into a personal anecdotal piece in a humorous self-mocking style which he had honed in many contributions to *Punch*, and sold it under the title of 'Nympholepsy' to the American magazine *Mademoiselle*, which paid a great deal more than *Punch*. Pocketing my share, I was impressed by this achievement – and perhaps a little piqued. It was then that I began to write humorous journalistic pieces of my own. Malcolm had a pragmatic, professional commitment to writing which was contagious. It was this basic, inexhaustible appetite for the craft and business of writing which, among other qualities, made him in due course such an inspiring teacher of younger writers. And he was always thrifty with ideas, aware that they do not grow on trees. In 1988 I encountered 'Nympholepsy' once again, much elaborated, revised and updated, in a chapter of his *Unsent Letters* (1988).

Close friendships between writers have a special character, especially when they are formed fairly early in their careers, when both parties are developing their work, showing it to each other, discussing it, perhaps collaborating on it. The friendship of Kingsley Amis and Philip Larkin was a classic example. Inevitably there is an element of competitiveness in such a relationship, which can cause some tension later, but at this early stage it is a constructive rivalry, as between two athletes specialising in the same events who train together. For three academic years, 1961–4, I enjoyed that kind of relationship with Malcolm continuously. We saw each other nearly every day at the university in term time, had offices on the same corridor, took coffee together in the senior common room and shared lunch in Staff House. There was always much to talk about: new books, new writing projects, departmental politics. It was a period of expansion and change in British universities, and the rather old-fashioned Birmingham syllabus was under revision, to make room, or more room, for areas of study in which Malcolm and I had an interest: modern English literature, American literature, literary theory. We started a seminar course for second- and third-year students called 'Comparative Critical Approaches' which we taught jointly. The name was coined by Richard Hoggart who was appointed as second Professor of

English Literature the year after Malcolm arrived and founded the Centre for Contemporary Cultural Studies, initially a postgraduate programme within the English Department, which would create a whole new subject in British higher education. Not all the more senior members of staff were enchanted with these develop-ments and department meetings could be long and contentious.

Our intimacy extended into social life, where Malcolm and Elizabeth soon became the principal friends and companions of Mary and myself, entertaining each other, going out to the cinema or the theatre and even, I recall, a black-tie staff dinner-dance, as one did in those days. They were better off than us – Malcolm, being older than me, was on a slightly higher salary, and was earning much more from his writing – and he owned a new VW Beetle, then a very trendy car, in which he drove us to the Royal Shakespeare Theatre in Stratford and other venues. He was a good, safe driver, and I remember him saying that it gave him great satisfaction because he had always been helpless and hopeless with anything mechanical. I envied him the car, and also the brand-new, centrally heated house he and Elizabeth bought in Edgbaston which compared favourably with the jerry-built two-bedroom inter-war semi we occupied in Selly Oak. But Malcolm's encouragement and example gave me hope that I could raise our standard of living with my pen in ways I had not considered before.

Several post-war British novelists began their careers with a 'day-job' teaching in a university, but most of them gave it up as soon as they felt able to do so. Malcolm and I were unusual in being equally committed and ambitious in our academic and creative careers. This was partly because the life of a freelance writer simply seemed too risky, especially for a married man with a family (Mary and I had two children by 1962 and the Bradburys had their first the following year) but it was also because we were genuinely interested in the academic study of literature, and wanted to make our mark on it. So we set ourselves up for a very busy life, combining teaching, writing scholarly books and articles, with writing novels, short stories, and in due course scripts for stage, radio and TV, as well as doing a good deal of journalism, including regular reviewing of new fiction, which in the 1960s was usually done in batches of half a dozen books at a time. We would not have been able to maintain this tempo of work if we had not married on the pre-Women's Lib assumption that the husband was the breadwinner whose work had priority and the woman the housewife and mother whose career was suspended during the early years of childbearing. It was symptomatic that I received the news that my second child, Stephen, had been born (four weeks earlier than expected) while attending a conference in London with Malcolm in the spring of 1962, and that when Elizabeth left the hospital with her first-born, Matthew, in the following year I drove her home in the clapped-out Ford Popular I had managed to acquire by then because Malcolm was away on some pre-arranged academic engagement.

Both Malcolm and I had grown up, like most of our generation, with a favourable image of America as our indispensable ally in the war, and as a land of greater affluence and opportunity than post-war Austerity Britain. In the 1960s its novelists seemed generally more innovative, and its academic critics more high-powered, than their British counterparts. Malcolm had spent two separate years in American universities before he came to Birmingham and he was planning to go back for another. What he said and wrote about America made me want to see it for myself. I applied for a Harkness Commonwealth Fellowship, a munificent scheme that no longer exists in the same form, which funded one or two years of study and travel in the United States for eligible candidates, and was lucky enough to be selected. In the late summer of 1964 I took a year's leave of absence from Birmingham and embarked on the *Queen Mary* with Mary and our children, aged four and two, for New York. I was attached to Brown University in Providence, Rhode Island for a semester, and spent the summer in San Francisco; in between we drove slowly across the country from east to west, and more quickly back again afterwards. My project was to educate myself in American literature, which I had never formally studied, but I also managed to write most of *The British Museum is Falling Down* and a short monograph on Graham Greene while I was there. It was an amazingly liberating and fulfilling year for me, and also for Mary, though the kids, especially Stephen, were too young to get much out of it.

In that age before email, fax machines and direct-dialling international telephone connections, Malcolm and I communicated by airmail letters or economical aerogrammes. I wrote more frequently, being free of mundane academic duties, he more copiously when he did find time to do so. I kept most of his letters and as I write this I have in front of me what was probably the first one he sent after our departure from Birmingham, headed simply 'Sunday' but evidently written in October 1964, which covers more than five sides of flimsy yellow quarto in single-spaced typescript. It begins with two pages of departmental news and gossip, then 'on the literary front, plenty of news too'. He had delivered his new novel, *Stepping Westward*, to Secker & Warburg and 'they were very pleased with it and . . . have offered what seems a much better advance – four hundred pounds . . .' It was to be published in the spring. 'They also want me to rewrite the Expatriates for them' (this was his PhD thesis) and '*Eating People* is going into its third Penguin edition'. His short book on Evelyn Waugh was coming out from Oliver & Boyd and he would send me a copy. He was delighted by my news that Doubleday had taken my second novel *Ginger, You're Barmy* for publication in America. He was planning another novel himself, and Bryan Wilson (a sociologist friend) had asked him to write a book for sixth-formers on the social background to literature (which he did in due course). Meanwhile 'I've done three scripts for *Swizzlewick* – a very interesting experience.' This was a twice-weekly BBC TV comedy drama series about the local council of a fictional Midlands town, created by the local playwright David Turner who had recently had a hit with a stage play called *Semi-Detached*. Turner wrote the first series, which had a mixed reception and aroused the ire of Mrs White-house; some other writers including Malcolm were co-opted to contribute to a second series.

The letter continued with proposals for my collaboration in new projects. The first was something called *Uncle Harvey*, of which I now retain no memory. It was evidently to be a kind of highbrow satirical radio revue for the Third Programme written by Malcolm, Jim Duckett (who had now graduated and was working as John Harrison's assistant at the Rep) and me, drawing on other writers like David Turner occasionally. Each programme would have a different theme, and Uncle Harvey was to be a linking character and presenter. Discussions with the BBC had gone well but they wanted to make a trial programme before committing themselves. (This programme, on the subject of British politics, written without my participation, was recorded in Birmingham, but nothing came of the project.) Malcolm reported that the script of *Between These Four Walls* had been sent to Ned Sherrin, producer of *That Was The Week That Was*, without eliciting any response, but John Harrison wanted us to do another revue for the Rep in the spring of 1963 – 'What do you think?' I didn't think I could collaborate at such a long distance, but the show, called *Slap in the Middle*, with additional input from David Turner, was postponed till the autumn of that year and I did contribute some material to it. I had been publishing some humorous pieces in American magazines and Malcolm asked me to keep them in a file so he could read them in due course, and he added as an afterthought: 'Oh, I have a piece coming up in *Mademoiselle* . . . You might see it!'

This letter gives some idea of Malcolm's extraordinary range of interests as a writer, his energy in pursuing them, and his infectious enthusiasm for collaboration, all qualities which made him such a stimulating friend to other writers. To my mind he often wasted his time on projects which had little hope of coming to fruition and some of which would bring him little money or prestige even if they did. But that was the way he worked: he liked to have lots of projects going at the same time and would drop them and pick them up again as circumstances dictated or allowed. More than thirty years passed before Secker finally published the book on American literary expatriates.

The last two paragraphs of the letter throw light on other aspects of his character. In the penultimate one he comments pessimistically on the result of the recent general election in England, which was won by Labour under Harold Wilson's leadership with a very narrow majority, after thirteen years of Tory government. I was surprised to be reminded of how right-wing Malcolm's views were, especially on education. 'I'm very miserable they got in,' he wrote. 'I've no doubt that if they stay in office long enough they'll ruin English universities . . . I feel the educational system will come in for a hell of a beating. Already in Bristol they are doing a great levelling act, cutting out the Direct Grant Schools.' Mary and I voted Labour and approved of comprehensive education, in which she had worked as a teacher, but this difference did not disturb our friendship with the Bradburys. I'm fairly sure he voted Liberal, not Conservative, in the '64 election, and later he was a vocal supporter of the SDP during its brief political life – as I was, less publicly. Ideologically he was a lower-case conservative, cherishing tradition, hierarchy, and moral principle. In the final paragraph of this letter he charmingly caricatured himself in this respect:

We are having a delightful time with Matthew, and the summer in Lockington was particularly enjoyable. I am growing quite doting; but then he is not either rebellious or sinful. I keep telling him about decent living, the high moral life, and respecting his father, and am encouraging him to go in for the church. Piety, piety I cry. I hope it works.

In February 1965 I received disturbing news from Malcolm. He was being headhunted by the new University of East Anglia at Norwich, who were luring him with the prospect of early promotion to Senior Lecturer and the chance to head and design an American Studies programme from scratch, and he was obviously tempted, though deeply divided, by the offer. He wrote: 'I'm in a state of great indecision: one thing it makes me realise is how attached I am to Birmingham, and how if I went I'd miss you.' I felt exactly the same, and wrote a letter setting out a number of reasons why he should stay in Birmingham, the final one being that he was a conservative as regards education and would be unhappy in an institution dedicated (as the 'New Universities' of that era were) to radical innovation in teaching the humanities. At the end of March, however, just as we were about to leave Providence, we heard that Malcolm had accepted UEA's offer. He told me long afterwards that on the day when he had promised to respond to it he went out with two letters in his pockets, one saying yes and one saying no, and posted the latter; but the next day UEA rang him up and said, 'You don't really mean it, do you?' and he agreed that he didn't. Malcolm hated to say no to anybody, as many people – literary editors, British Council officers, conference convenors, and secretaries of literary societies – discovered to their advantage.

I wrote back, only slightly exaggerating the note of grief. 'Oh Malcolm, how could you do it? How could you turn your back on Brum and us? We're really very desolated that you won't be there when we get back.' Communication was interrupted during our long trek west, and it wasn't until May that I received from Malcolm a fuller account of the matter and his fluctuating feelings about it. Apparently Richard Hoggart had suggested to Terence Spencer that he should see if Birmingham could match Norwich's offer with something comparable, and Spencer, after seeming receptive to the idea, had finally failed to act on it. 'This very complicated situation has involved us in all kinds of doubts, anguish and uncertainty, and is half a reason for our excessive silence, since in a way I was hoping that I'd still be in Birmingham after all. I shall feel particularly depressed about not having your day-to-day company. This won't mean that we won't see each other, obviously, but less often, and not teaching together, which will be a great loss.'

And of course we did continue to see each other at regular intervals over the years that followed, sometimes on academic occasions, sometimes on visits with wives and children. We had a two-family holiday in Brittany together in 1967, and much later a touring holiday without children in the same part of France. When

Malcolm and Angus Wilson (who had a part-time post at UEA) started the MA course in creative writing there, which under Malcolm's direction would become the most successful of its kind in the country, I was its first external examiner. (There was only one student that year, Ian McEwan. I wish I could say I instantly recognised his genius, but I didn't, though I did pass him, complaining of the scruffy state of his manuscripts.) In 1977 Malcolm encouraged me to apply for the Henfield Fellowship in creative writing at UEA which was associated with the MA course, and I spent a summer term there writing part of *How Far Can You Go?*, living in a little maisonette on campus and occupying Malcolm's office, as he was on sabbatical leave. Since he was working at home I saw a good deal of him and spent every Sunday with the family. And for twenty years or more we would meet every July at the British Council Seminar in Cambridge, previously mentioned, at which I was a regular guest speaker, as was Malcolm himself after he handed over the chairmanship to his friend and colleague at UEA, Christopher Bigsby.

There were fewer reasons to tempt Malcolm to revisit Birmingham, but among them was television. He was one of the first English literary novelists to embrace the medium enthusiastically, and he kept faith with it throughout his career, in spite of many frustrations and disappointments. The BBC's Drama Department at Pebble Mill in Birmingham was a centre of innovative production until it was phased out at the turn of the century; Malcolm had made contacts with the people who worked there when he lived in the city and maintained them after he left. The first fruit of this association

was a 'Play for Today' broadcast in January 1975 called
The After Dinner Game which he wrote (characteristically)
in collaboration with Chris Bigsby. It was a studio play,
as most TV drama was in those days, rehearsed like a
stage play and then recorded on video by a multi-camera
method in twenty-minute 'takes', which had to be
aborted and done again from the beginning if anyone
fluffed their lines. I went along to Pebble Mill at
Malcolm's invitation to watch this tense, complicated,
collaborative operation, impressed by, and a little envious
of, his involvement in it. The experience kindled in me
a desire to get involved myself one day, though it was
many years before that came to pass, by which time TV
drama had become less theatrical and more filmic, and
Malcolm had demonstrated his professional mastery of
the medium in numerous original plays, mini-series, and
adaptations. Like every writer who works in television
and film, he wrote many scripts that were never
produced, but he was exceptionally unlucky with the
adaptation of his own novel, *Rates of Exchange*, which
the BBC commissioned him to write as a six-part serial.
Two weeks before principal photography was due to
begin (on location in Hungary) when it was, of course,
fully cast, and several hundreds of thousands of pounds
had already been spent on it, the project was cancelled
because of a dispute, or crisis, over budgeting in the
BBC's Drama Department. Only someone who has been
professionally involved in television drama, and knows
how difficult it is to get a major serial 'green-lighted'
for production, and has some idea of how much rewriting
of the screenplay is demanded even after that point has
been reached, can begin to imagine the depth of

Malcolm's disappointment. Many writers would have given up the medium in disgust, but he persevered with it, pausing only to relieve his feelings in a satirical novella, *Cuts* (1987).

It is clear from our correspondence in 1965 that we both genuinely mourned our separation, and if I had been in Birmingham at the time I would undoubtedly have done more to persuade Malcolm to stay there. But in retrospect it was obviously essential for our individual development as writers that we should separate. One department could hardly contain two novelists writing satirical academic novels, and it was necessary that we should have different experiences to draw on for them. *Changing Places* and *The History Man* both appeared in the same year, 1975, and both were about the same basic phenomenon – the global radicalisation of universities in the late 1960s/early 1970s – but observed in very different places and fictionalised in quite different ways. I was right in predicting that Malcolm would find aspects of the radical ethos of UEA uncongenial, but that was precisely what provoked his masterpiece, *The History Man*. Like Evelyn Waugh, whose work he admired enormously, Malcolm's imagination responded with gleeful relish to the things in contemporary society he found most alien, extreme and absurd.

Changing Places was inspired by an appointment as Visiting Associate Professor at the University of California in Berkeley in the first half of 1969, a time when it was a key site of the student revolution and 1960s' counterculture. I was determined to make use of this material

in a novel, but conscious that several novels had already
been published about visiting Englishmen having trans-
forming experiences in American universities, not least
Malcolm's *Stepping Westward* (1965), in which a provincial
British novelist called James Walker is writer-in-residence
at a campus in the middle of America and proves ill-
equipped to read the political plot in which he becomes
involved. Pondering how to find some new angle on
this transatlantic rite of passage, it occurred to me that
there had been no novels about American academics
visiting British universities, though this was not un-
common in those days, usually through an exchange
scheme. That was how the binary structure of *Changing
Places* – two professors, one English and one American,
having parallel adventures in each other's habitats –
evolved, partly out of the need to differentiate my work
from Malcolm's.

To my surprise and disappointment the novel was
turned down by three publishers before Malcolm, who
had read it with appreciation, recommended that I send
it to his own publisher, Tom Rosenthal at Secker &
Warburg. We already had the same literary agent,
Graham Watson of Curtis Brown, to whom Malcolm
had introduced me soon after we first met, and he acted
on Malcolm's suggestion. Tom Rosenthal accepted the
novel, subject to some reduction in length. When it was
published it received a royal flush of good reviews and
my fortunes as a novelist improved dramatically. I have
published my novels with Secker (now Harvill Secker)
ever since. Many authors would have hesitated to encourage a writer-friend whose work in various ways
inevitably competed with theirs to join their own

publisher's list, but Malcolm's helpful gesture was typically generous and unselfish. In the late autumn of 1975 Tom Rosenthal told us he had been informed by the *Yorkshire Post* that they had narrowed the choice for their annual Fiction Prize to *Changing Places* and *The History Man*. When my novel won Malcolm's disappointment must have been sharpened by the irony that he had been instrumental in getting it published, but he never exhibited any hard feelings. It was a minor prize, only £150 in value, but it was a first for me and would have been for him. Happily a few months later he received the Royal Society of Literature's Heinemann Award for *The History Man*. Neither novel, incidentally, was shortlisted for the Booker Prize that year, when the judges decided that only two novels instead of the usual six were worthy of the honour. One of the judges was Angus Wilson, who told Malcolm privately that he had felt unable to argue for *The History Man* because they were colleagues at UEA, but it is more probable that he disliked the book's take on contemporary culture.

In the next decade the Booker Prize became much more important in determining rewards and reputations – some would say excessively so. From 1980 onwards the choice of the winner was postponed until the day of the banquet at which it was announced, an event covered live on television. These developments allowed bookmakers to accept bets on the result and converted the event into a kind of literary Oscar night, steeply raising its public profile. In 1982 Malcolm was chairman of the panel that awarded the prize to Salman Rushdie for *Midnight's Children* (though he told me his own preference was for D.M. Thomas's *The White Hotel*).

The following year he was shortlisted for his own novel, *Rates of Exchange*, about an English academic's adventures on a British Council lecture tour in an imaginary East European country under communist rule called Slaka. A few days before the banquet I sent him a postcard wishing him good luck, a picture of James Joyce as a young man looking quizzically into the lens of the camera. (When asked what he was thinking at that moment Joyce said he was wondering if the photographer would lend him five shillings.) The prize, however, went to J.M. Coetzee for *Life & Times of Michael K*. I phoned Malcolm next day to commiserate, and he said to me at the end of the conversation, in a tone at once encouraging and wistful, 'Now it's your turn', knowing that I would have a new novel out next year. *Small World*, a carnivalesque romance about the international conference scene, was indeed shortlisted in 1984, when the surprise winner was Anita Brookner, for *Hotel du Lac*. At the end of my story, which was set in 1979, most of the characters are brought together at the huge annual convention of the American Modern Language Association in New York, and I contrived a brief Hitchcockian appearance in these pages for Malcolm and myself at a VIP cocktail party. The young hero of the tale overhears in the throng 'a shortish, dark-haired man . . . talking to a tallish dark-haired man smoking a pipe. "If I can have Eastern Europe," the tallish man was saying in an English accent, "you can have the rest of the world." "All right," said the shortish man, "but I daresay people will still get us mixed up."'

And of course they did. I was once telephoned in my Birmingham office by a man who asked me to settle a bet that I was the same person as Malcolm Bradbury. Letters were often addressed to me at the University of East Anglia, including one from the Rupert Murdoch Professor of Communications at Oxford. We were interviewed together by a German radio journalist at some British Council event in Hamburg and I vividly remember the panic on her face as she realised halfway through that she had mixed up our identities. Writing about this incident in a newspaper column I said we were in danger of becoming the Rosencrantz and Guildenstern of contemporary English letters. The continual confusion was amusing but also exasperating. In spite of generic resemblances between some of our novels, it seemed to us that most of them were quite distinct in technique and thematic preoccupations.

When *Nice Work* was shortlisted for the Booker prize in 1988, Malcolm was among the distinguished guests at the final banquet who, as they arrived at the Mansion House, were quizzed on live television about who should or would win, and I watched a video-recording of the event next day, in a hungover and somewhat despondent mood induced by having been a runner-up once again. Tall and handsome in his dinner jacket, Malcolm said with a smile, 'For love and friendship, I hope it's David Lodge', for which I blessed him, knowing that such an outcome would have revived the hurt of his own disappointment five years earlier. The element of rivalry which was always inevitably present in our relationship had by now become a potential threat to its stability, and we preserved our friendship by surrendering some of the intimacy of the early years. We no longer discussed our writing plans in detail or showed each other work in progress or gave detailed critiques of the novels when they were published, limiting ourselves to supportive expressions of general approval. I think we both wished to avoid getting too close to each other's work, perhaps being influenced by it through knowing too much about it, and thus encouraging the people who insisted on pairing us together or confusing us with each other. But this is not to say that influence ceased. As Mikhail Bakhtin observed, all writers glance sideways at their peers as they write, and it was Malcolm whom I most often invoked as imagined reader and critic, to test the quality of the work.

Our last collaboration, if it can be called that, was a Foreword/Afterword I wrote for a characteristic production of Malcolm's, *My Strange Quest for Mensonge: Structuralism's Hidden Hero* published by Secker in 1987. This started life as an article published in the *Observer* on 1 April 1984, which described a seminally important text called *La Fornication comme acte culturel* by an obscure French literary intellectual called Henri Mensonge, parodying and travestying the jargon of Continental literary theory in the process. It fooled a considerable number of readers, who failed to notice that the surname means 'lie' in French. Later Malcolm developed it into a short book and Tom Rosenthal asked if I would write an appropriate Foreword or Afterword. I wrote it in the persona of Michel Tardieu, the French Professor of Structuralist Narratology who was a character in *Small World*. He finds the identity of the nominal author of the book as suspiciously elusive as its subject:

There is a suggestive consonance between the syllables 'Bradbury' and 'Bunbury', perhaps the most famous *alias* in the pages of English literature, which persuades me that the name is a floating signifier that has attached itself to many discrete signifieds: Bradbury the campus novelist, Bradbury the Professor of American Studies, Bradbury the Booker Prize judge, Bradbury the TV adapter of postmodernist novelists like John Fowles and Tom Sharpe, Bradbury the tireless international conference-goer and British Council Lecturer. Even within those disparate categories there is doubt and difficulty in establishing the facts – many British readers, for instance, being convinced that the novels of Malcolm Bradbury are written by David Lodge, and *vice versa*.

I had been a half-time professor at Birmingham since 1984, and around the time that *Mensonge* was published I took early retirement from my post at Birmingham to become a full-time freelance writer. Malcolm carried on at UEA as Professor of American Studies till 1995, but with reduced duties, concentrating increasingly on the MA programme in creative writing, which by now commanded tremendous prestige, and continuing to appear in all the guises listed by Tardieu. Each of us decided at about the same time to steer our narrative writing in a new direction, and we took the same generic route: the biographical novel about a classic writer. My *Author, Author* was written after Malcolm's death, but I first made a note about the relationship between Henry James and George Du Maurier as a possible subject for a novel in 1995, before I discovered that Malcolm was writing a novel about Denis Diderot, the French encyclopaedist, versatile man of letters and prominent figure of the Enlightenment, whose wide-ranging intellectual energy Malcolm admired, and whose disappointments stirred his sympathies. As soon as *To the Hermitage* was finished he began to plan a novel about Chateaubriand's visit to America in 1791–2, a fragment of which gave *Liar's Landscape* its title; and after writing *Author, Author* I decided to write a novel about H.G. Wells. Our earlier novels had all been set in our own lifetimes. We were, of course, part of a cultural trend: towards the end of the last century and in the first decade of the present one an increasing number of literary novelists published books which applied the techniques of fiction to the life stories of past writers. But it is interesting that we were both attracted quite independently to this kind of project at the same stage of our careers. And different as they are, *To the Hermitage* and *Author, Author* have some features in common: both end with the death of the main character, and both contain reflections on what Malcolm's narrator calls 'Postmortemism' – whether, for instance, the life of books after their authors' deaths compensates for the disappointments and frustrations of a literary vocation, or indeed for the irreducible fact of death itself. In *To the Hermitage* this theme is explored in a variety of ways, including a number of humorous anecdotes about the bizarre or mysterious fates of the actual corpses of writers such as Descartes, Voltaire and, most importantly, Lawrence Sterne. The author of *Tristram Shandy* and *A Sentimental Journey* was as much a source of inspiration for Malcolm's book as Diderot, for he spliced together a rambling, digressive, Shandean narrative of his own pilgrimage to St Petersburg in 1993, with an account of Diderot's residence there as the guest of Catherine the Great in 1773–4.

To the Hermitage was published in the early summer of 2000. Its moving conclusion, describing Diderot's decline and death on his return to Paris, acquired an additional poignancy for readers from Malcolm's death in November of the same year. The new millennium had begun well for him with the bestowal of a knighthood, but that was quickly overshadowed by illness and the diagnosis of a rare respiratory disease which did not respond to the usual treatment. He struggled to carry out the programme of events arranged that summer to promote To the Hermitage, and had to cancel several of them, his misery increased by some wounding reviews of the novel. (Malcolm himself published hundreds of reviews in his life, and I don't remember ever reading a destructive one.) When I saw him in October he was confined to a bed that had been set up in his study, and deeply depressed. He said 'I'm beginning to think I'm not going to get over this', and although of course I demurred, I was not confident that he would. Imagining how enviably happy and healthy I must seem to him, and how I would feel in his situation, I pitied him from the bottom of my heart. His condition rapidly deteriorated and on 27 November he died in a hospice, with Elizabeth and their two sons beside him. The news was a shock to the literary world, for, by his own wish, few people had been made aware of how ill he was.

There was a private funeral early in December, and a memorial service in Norwich Cathedral in February of the new year attended by 500 people, an indication of how sadly Malcolm was missed by friends, colleagues and collaborators in many different walks of life. I spoke on that occasion, and I concluded my address with these words:

> Another writer-friend gave me a diary at the beginning of last year, with a hand-written passage or sketch by a writer or artist on every page. The passage for the day of Malcolm's funeral, Monday 4th December, had in one sense an uncanny appropriateness. It was contributed by the Irish novelist Brian Moore, who must have written it not long before his own death, and it was a quotation from Roland Barthes' essay on Chateaubriand. As many of you will know, Malcolm was working on a novel about Chateaubriand when he died. The quotation is: 'Memory is the beginning of writing and writing is, in its turn, the beginning of death.' But if I understand that correctly – and Barthes is an elusive writer – I don't really agree with it. It has always seemed to me that writing is a kind of defiance of death, because our books live on after we have gone. Certainly the greatest consolation we have for Malcolm's passing is that we can re-experience his company, his character, and his life-enhancing sense of fun, through his books. But that is not the same, of course, as a living, breathing, laughing friend.

The laughing is important. Ian McEwan has recalled that 'It was part of Malcolm's automatic generosity to laugh easily at other people's jokes. Who can forget that delighted, whinnying giggle?' People liked to be in his company because he generated a life-enhancing effort of mutual amusement. When I wrote the article on him for the *New Oxford Dictionary of National Biography* the editor asked me to add to my first draft, which was an account of his life and career, a description of his personal appearance and bearing, and this is what I wrote:

> Physically Bradbury was tall, but never used his height to intimidate. His manners were gentle, his voice light. His speech had no perceptible class or regional accent, though in later life it acquired an attractive, slightly patrician drawl. When he read from his own work his delivery had a distinctive rising and falling intonation. He possessed a whole spectrum of laughs, from an infectious giggle to a full-throated guffaw. His long, handsome face, surmounted by dark wavy hair that became thinner and grizzled in later years, was the face of an intellectual, the broad brow furrowed with the traces of thought; but there were laughlines around the eyes and the mouth was always apt to break into a smile. When he wrote on the typewriter or computer, the tip of his tongue flickered and curled between his lips as if in sympathy with the difficulty and delicacy of the task.

THE DEATH OF DIANA

This is an edited version of an essay written two or three weeks after the death of Diana, Princess of Wales on 31 August 1997. I wrote it 'on spec', mainly because I wanted to record my own impressions of, and thoughts about, the event and its aftermath while they were still fresh in my mind. I vaguely hoped to place it in an American or foreign journal, but by the time it was finished the international press was sated with articles on this subject, and I soon abandoned the attempt. Later I made some use of the material in a stage play and a novella entitled Home Truths. *In 2001 I donated the essay to an anthology called* Sightlines, *published to support the Royal National Institute for the Blind's Talking Books Appeal. I shortened the original text considerably, but left its reflections as they were expressed in September 1997, and it is reprinted in that form here.*

I heard the news relatively late, because we don't listen to the radio at home in the mornings, and there was nothing about it in the Sunday papers delivered to our provincial doorstep. I was in the kitchen making mid-morning coffee, timed for the return of my wife from attending mass at our Roman Catholic parish church. I usually accompanied her, but on this occasion I hadn't.

Mary came in at about half-past ten, frowning. 'Have you heard that Princess Diana has died?' she said. 'There were prayers for her at mass.' I think I said, 'Oh no!' – something like that, anyway. I remember feeling an unexpectedly sharp pang of real regret, quite different from what one usually feels about the death of a well-known but remote public figure. 'How?' was my first question. Mary didn't know. She hadn't lingered at the church to enquire because we were going out, to a horticultural sale at a country house north of Birmingham.

We turned on the television and learned the basic facts about the accident in Paris. We watched and listened to the Prime Minister speaking live outside his parish church in County Durham. He looked genuinely shocked and grief-stricken. The reporters and presenters on TV also seemed exceptionally moved by what they were reporting, real feeling threatening to overwhelm their professionalism. Martyn Lewis's voice broke once and it seemed to me that his cheeks were wet. This struck me as extraordinary and unprecedented. But there didn't seem to be any immediate prospect of additional hard news, only speculation and handwringing. We decided to go ahead with our expedition, but we talked over the tragedy in the car, and during the rest of the outing. Again and again one's thoughts kept reverting to it. My predominant reaction, after that initial, surprising pang of personal regret, the simple wish that it hadn't happened, was to reflect on the extraordinarily *literary* quality of the manner and timing of Diana's death. No novelist or scriptwriter could have improved on its ironies and symmetries: the legendary princess cut down in her prime, together with the man recently acknowledged as the love of her life, apparently hounded to death by the lackeys of the very media which had made her famous. The day was dark and rainy, and we drove home in the early afternoon in a ferocious thunderstorm, as if nature was doing its best to encourage the pathetic fallacy. I thought of *Julius Caesar*: 'When beggars die, there are no comets seen; / The heavens themselves blaze forth the death of princes.'

As soon as we got indoors I switched on the television, just in time to see Prince Charles arriving at the Paris hospital with Diana's two shocked-looking sisters. From then onwards it was hard to keep away from the television. I had never met the princess, nor seen her in the flesh; I had never thought about her unless she was prominently in the news (which admittedly had been quite often, especially over the last few weeks) and I had always regarded her as a flawed human being – more sinned against than sinning, certainly, but at least partly responsible for her own misfortunes, and excessively concerned with her own public image. And yet I felt that a light had gone out of the world. I was not alone. It soon became clear that the whole nation, or a very large part of it, was swamped by an extraordinarily powerful tidal wave of emotion, in which grief predominated.

Diana's death and the events of the week following surely constituted one of the most extraordinary public dramas of the twentieth century, a collective catharsis that climaxed at the funeral – especially at that moment, beyond the daring of any scriptwriter's imagination,

when applause on the streets of London for the Earl
Spencer's broadcast eulogy, with its implicit criticism of
the Royal Family, surged through the open doors of the
abbey and was taken up by the congregation. In Hyde
Park, more than 100,000 people who were watching
the funeral service on giant TV screens, many in tears,
leapt to their feet and clapped their hands. A friend of
mine who was there, the theatre and film director Mike
Ockrent, told me it was an electrifying experience. 'I
understood for the first time the nature of a revolutionary
crowd,' he said. 'If somebody had told us to march
against Buckingham Palace, we would have marched.'
But those commentators who dismissed the whole thing
as a product of mass hysteria or media manipulation
seem to me to have completely misread it. It was
authentic.

Literally millions of blossoms – weighing some 10,000
tons in all, it is estimated – were gathered and laid upon
the ground in Diana's memory. A charitable fund opened
in her name quickly attracted over £100 million in
donations. Her place of burial is expected to become a
popular shrine. There is talk of constructing a 'pilgrimage
walk' through the London parks connecting landmarks
associated with her life. Hardbitten journalists have apolo-
gised in print for the snide articles they wrote about her
in the past. My wife, summarising one such *mea culpa*
to me at breakfast, suddenly burst into tears, surprising
herself as much as me. Three Scottish professional foot-
ballers, a social group not renowned for emotional
sensitivity, flatly refused to play for their country in an
international match scheduled for the day of Diana's
funeral, and forced the Scottish Football Association to

change the date of the fixture. My tennis club closed for the morning of the funeral, but reopened at 2 p.m. The organiser of social tennis, a down-to-earth forty-something Birmingham businessman, sent a message that he was 'too upset' to attend. A man told a national phone-in radio programme that he had lost his wife through cancer last April; they had been happily married for forty-four years and he loved her dearly, but he had shed more tears for Diana than for his wife. These are just a few representative facts and anecdotes culled from thousands.

Whether the effects of Diana's death prove to be lasting or ephemeral, the public and private reaction to it, not only in Britain but around the world, was extraordinary, and the question remains: why? Many theories have been advanced in the last few weeks. None of them alone can explain the phenomenon; but perhaps when considered together they begin to suggest an answer to the question. I list them as versions of Diana and interpretations of her 'meaning'.

1. The Star

'She was a star.' The term was used again and again in the immediate aftermath of Diana's death. Once restricted to the movie industry, it is now applied to celebrities of all kinds. In the secularised modern world, stars are the nearest thing we have to the pagan deities of old, after one of whom Diana herself was named. Stars are like us, and sometimes they visit our mundane world and touch our lives, but mostly they inhabit another plane of existence, a world of luxury, glamour, mobility and excess, which we can only glimpse through the media. Nobody is born a star, but some achieve stardom and some have it thrust upon them. Diana belonged to the latter category. What propelled her from obscurity to fame was of course her engagement and marriage to the heir to the British throne. It was, as people said at the time, a fairy-tale wedding, a modern Cinderella story. Her good fortune seemed to demonstrate that the wish-fulfilment of romance need not be confined to the world of fiction; it could actually happen. In fact Diana belonged to a rich and aristocratic family, and had had the conventional upbringing of a girl of her class. But at the time of her engagement she *seemed* like the girl next door – pretty, shy, unaffected and unpretentious, earning her living in a humble job (assistant at a nursery school) and sharing a flat with other working girls. She was seen as a catalyst that would modernise and humanise the monarchy.

As we all know, that hope was dashed, and the fairy-tale turned into something more melodramatic and more ironic: the royal soap-opera. It is important to remember, amid the posthumous adulation she is receiving, that public opinion was always divided about Diana's part in the deterioration and collapse of her marriage to Charles, and about her behaviour after they separated and divorced. If she had lived to marry her Dodi, she would undoubtedly have attracted a good deal of criticism for so doing. Controversy didn't make her any less of a star – on the contrary – but it was only in death that she achieved apotheosis, that immortal stardom which very few, such as Marilyn Monroe, Eva Peron and Elvis

Presley have attained – and none of them on the same global scale. Diana's death instantly edited out all her faults and follies in public consciousness. It was only her virtues, her good works, her suffering and her beauty that were remembered. In the days following her death we were frequently told that she had been the most famous woman in the world, and it seemed obviously true, but I can't recall anyone saying it before she died.

2. The Icon

It is hardly necessary to state that Diana would never have achieved her quasi-mythical status if she hadn't been beautiful, but it is worth considering what kind of beauty it was, and how it was mediated. It was not flawless (her nose, for instance, was too long and the wrong shape for classical perfection) but it was highly photogenic. In the days following her death we were reminded again and again of the stunning visual impact of her appearance in photographs and on film. To use a movie industry cliché, the camera loved her; while, as a writer in the *Independent* newspaper shrewdly observed, portrait painters generally failed to convey any sense of her exceptional physical presence. She could have been a model – she had the tall, lissom figure for it, and the natural grace of movement, and a passion for clothes. Though she suffered from and resented the attentions of the *paparazzi*, she clearly enjoyed posing for the camera on her own terms.

Cynics will say that Diana's fame was precisely an illusion, a trick performed by the media, who exploited her iconic potential for their own materialistic ends; and that the demonstration of public grief at her death was also largely generated and manipulated by the same agencies. Undoubtedly the myth of Diana both before and after her death would never have developed as it did before the age of the mass media. It was through them that she imprinted her image on our consciousness, more deeply than we realised until she was dead. But the media are such an all-pervasive part of modern life that it is vain to suppose we can find some other, more authentic ground for public, collective experience. Although there was certainly something contagious about the grieving for Diana which television, in particular, encouraged, there was nothing hysterical about the behaviour of the people who queued to write in the books of condolence, or lined the streets of Diana's funeral route. And the saturation coverage of the event does not explain, or explain away, the small private pang of sorrow which most people felt when they first heard the news.

3. The Madonna of the Charities

The media that were so pruriently fascinated by Diana's marital and emotional problems in life have focused since her death on her devotion to her two sons, and on her work for charity and good causes like the abolition of anti-personnel mines. This is all part of the ongoing secular canonisation of Diana, against which the Earl Spencer gently warned in his funeral address, when he pointed out that her high-profile charitable work was

in part an effort to overcome a lack of self-esteem. This
is not to say that it was simply a calculated polishing of
her public image. On the contrary it is clear that she
often did good by stealth, and that when she did it
publicly she genuinely saw this as a way of turning her
media celebrity to positive account. However, it was,
again, her beauty, her effortless physical grace, which
made her such a potent figure in the fund-raising,
consciousness-raising business. The images we saw
replayed and reprinted again and again in the weeks after
her death, of Diana touching an AIDS patient, of Diana
walking through a minefield, and above all of Diana
hugging, cradling and holding on her lap children and
infants suffering from all kinds of dreadful disease, muti-
lation and malnutrition, were intensely moving precisely
because she never seemed to be straining for effect. She
didn't need to.

4. The Culture-Heroine

I borrow this term from the American folklorist Richard
Chase's classic essay, 'The Brontës, or Myth Domesticated'
first published in the *Kenyon Review* in 1947, and often
reprinted:

> Rochester and Heathcliff are portrayed as being
> at once godlike and satanic. In them the universal
> enemies may be set at war by a culture-heroine.
> Then if the Devil is overcome, a higher state of
> society will have been achieved. The tyrannical
> Father-God will have been displaced.

Chase argued that the Brontë sisters, or their fictional heroines, ultimately backed away from the achievement of this mission, settling for domesticity, bourgeois marriage and Christian orthodoxy; but he gave them credit for challenging their patriarchal society in such ambitious terms, anticipating later feminist interpretation of their work.

Feminist writers have been ambivalent about Diana, especially Diana the star and Diana the icon, for obvious reasons; but many women in Britain today, and in other countries, have seen her struggle for personal fulfilment against the restrictions imposed on her by a monarchy whose values are essentially patriarchal (even though the present monarch is a queen), and her experience of emotional neglect, marital breakdown, depression, eating disorders and single parenthood, as an epic version of their own trials and tribulations. The key to the astonishing reaction to Diana's death, according to the psychologist Oliver James, writing in the *Independent*, 'was the way that the agonies of her particular plotline mirrored the real suffering of the populace, particularly women and young people . . . above all, the scale of the reaction is caused by a massive undercurrent of misery that afflicts women throughout the developed world today and for which Diana's death is a conduit'. It is crucial to this interpretation that Diana was killed at the very moment when she seemed to have eluded the repressive patriarchal forces ranged against her. If she had married Dodi and spent the rest of her life swanning happily about the world in luxury yachts and private planes from one exclusive fleshpot to another, she would have failed as a culture-heroine even more spectacularly than Chase thought the Brontë heroines failed.

This is not merely a feminist issue. Much has been read by political commentators into the mass identification with Diana in her death by people of all races, creeds and classes in British society, and their success in forcing a full-scale ceremony of public mourning upon a reluctant Royal Family. It has been dubbed the 'Floral Revolution' by Martin Jacques, former editor of *Marxism Today*. Jacques was one of the first British Marxist intellectuals to recognise that the Thatcher era had banished old-fashioned socialism from British political life for good, and that New Labour's version of a market economy humanised by a corporate state was the left's best hope for the future. Connections have been drawn between Tony Blair's landslide victory last May and the surge of popular feeling over the death of Diana, reinforced by the Prime Minister's faultless handling of the latter event, publicly and behind the scenes.

The general election result and the popular reaction to Diana's death were both unprecedented and totally unexpected in *scale*; and both were motivated by sentiment rather than ideology. The occurrence of two such massive convulsions in such a short space of time has prompted speculation that British society really has changed; that the old patriarchal code of the stiff upper lip, emotional reticence, respect for authority, tradition and social precedence, which used to characterise us as a nation, has gone for ever, along with the cynicism, individualism and greed which flourished in the Thatcher years, to be replaced by a much more open, flexible and compassionate and feminised ethos. Well, we shall see.

5. The Victim

The first instinctive reaction to Diana's death was to see her as the victim of a degenerate press, and this remains an important element in the more complex web of emotion and interpretation that now surrounds the event. It would have been deeply satisfying to the general public if early reports that the *paparazzi* directly caused the fatal accident by buzzing her car on their motorcycles had been confirmed. It now seems clear that the main cause was that the driver Henri Paul was drunk (and using pharmaceutical drugs prescribed for depression and alcoholism) and driving the vehicle at reckless speed. Indirectly, however, the *paparazzi were* responsible for the tragedy. Their relentless pursuit of Diana and Dodi, which had been going on for weeks, had reached a pitch of hysteria on both sides by the day of the fatal crash. An article in the London *Sunday Times* for 7 September which reconstructed the last day of Diana and Dodi in meticulous detail, revealed that the couple changed their plans several times in a vain effort to throw the photographers off their trail. And the well-attested reports of the *paparazzi* clustered round the crushed Mercedes like carrion crows, shooting photos of the dead and dying occupants through the windows instead of giving assistance, aroused widespread anger and disgust. Here, at the scene of her death, the various images of Diana – the divinity, the icon, the culture-heroine, the victim – were violently forced together. The Earl Spencer noted in his tribute the irony that his sister, named after the goddess of hunting, was herself the most hunted of human beings. But another legend associated with the goddess

Diana – the story of Actaeon surprising her bathing – portrays her as the object of male voyeurism. The *paparazzi*, toting their gross telescopic lenses like swollen phalluses, are the very embodiment of commercialised voyeurism. There have been calls for new laws and codes of practice to restrict their activities, and promises by contrite editors not to use their services in future. But I fear this will be the most transitory effect of Diana's death.

6. The Departed Soul

If Richard Dawkins has publicly commented on the death of Diana and its aftermath, I missed it. I would dearly like to know what he, or Daniel Dennett, or any other of our fashionable neo-Darwinian scientists and philosophers, made of it. They must be exasperated. For years they have been telling us in well-written, well-argued, well-researched books and articles and lectures and TV documentaries that there is no such thing as the immortal soul, no ghost in the machine; that individual self-consciousness is a product of the brain capacity we happen to have surplus to our evolutionary requirements, and ceases when our brain activity ceases; that human beings are disposable vehicles for the transmission of genes, the only true immortals. Then a beautiful young woman dies in a car crash and all over the world people are consumed with grief, and seek consolation in behaviour that, however vulgar and improvised, has its roots in religious ritual and language and assumes the immortality of the individual soul. Anyone who had stood up in Hyde Park on Saturday 6 September and declared

that the person called Diana, Princess of Wales, was
extinguished utterly and for ever would have been seriously endangering their health. 'DIANA WE LOVE YOU'
was inscribed on a banner held up during the minute's
silence at an international football match between
England and Moldova ten days after her death. Not
'loved' but 'love'. Diana lives.

But is this a manifestation of unsuspected reservoirs
of faith, or a release of suppressed anxiety and dread?
Britain today is a largely secular country, with a small
and diminishing number of regular churchgoers. And
among the latter many, like myself, unwilling to sever
their links with that long and rich tradition of scripture,
liturgy and ethical discourse which has contributed so
much to human civilisation, will readily admit that for
them it only makes a kind of metaphorical sense,
expressing a yearning for, rather than a belief in, transcendence. The scientific materialists are much more
confident, and more plausible. We fear they may be
right. Science has not deprived us of awe and wonder
at the nature of the universe – quite the contrary; but
it has made the idea of a personal God who intervenes
in human history, and numbers every hair of our individual heads, desperately difficult to believe for all except
fundamentalists. Immortality seems impossible; but
extinction seems unbearable. That is the existential
double-bind in which we find ourselves.

The man, or woman, in the street does not perhaps
reflect on these matters in such abstract terms, but the
same unresolved contradiction gnaws away at their
peace of mind, as they pursue the materialistic good
life which capitalism and modern technology have

made increasingly accessible. We all live in secret fear
of the positive biopsy, the unsurvivable air-crash, the
fatal road accident, that interrupts and renders irrelevant
our quotidian desires, anxieties and satisfactions. When
we hear about such things happening to strangers, or
read about them in the newspapers, or see them on
the TV news, our compassion is mingled with relief
that the tragedy didn't happen to us, or anyone near
and dear to us, and with the dread knowledge that one
day it will, in one form or another. We quickly suppress
these intimations of mortality, and get on with our
lives. But when the tragedy happens to a star, a goddess,
an icon, a culture-heroine, a figure uniquely loaded
with meanings for a vast number of people, who seemed
to move on a different plane from ordinary mortals,
but succumbed to the most banal and unnecessary of
violent deaths, then it is not surprising if all that
repressed emotion should erupt in an explosion of
collective grief and quasi-religious feeling. The man
who wept more for Diana than for his wife was perhaps
only weeping deferred tears for his spouse, and proleptic
tears for his own inevitable end.

> *Margaret, are you grieving*
> *Over Goldengrove unleaving?*

Thus begins Gerard Manley Hopkins's poem, 'Spring
and Fall', addressed to a young child moved to tears by
the sad beauty of the autumn leaves. It ends:

> *It is the blight man was born for,*
> *It is Margaret you mourn for.*

In the last analysis it was not Diana, but ourselves, that we mourned for.

September 1997

TROLLOPE'S FIXED PERIOD

A NTHONY TROLLOPE PUBLISHED his first novel in
1847 when he was thirty-one, and went on to write
forty-five more, and some twenty-five other books,
including five collections of short stories, before his
death in 1882, an average of two books a year over
thirty-five years. For the first twenty years of this prolific
literary career he had a responsible full-time position in
the Post Office, supervising and improving the postal
service in various regions of Ireland and England. He
was also a keen horseman, and seized every opportunity
to hunt until age restricted him to merely riding. After
he moved back from Ireland to England he was an active
member of several London clubs, including the Athe-
naeum and the Garrick. When he finally resigned from
the Post Office he immediately took on the editorship
of a magazine, and later he stood unsuccessfully as Liberal
candidate for Beverley in a general election. If he had
become a Member of Parliament, we can be sure he
would have continued to write novels. How he achieved
his astonishing output of books while leading such a full
life was revealed in his posthumously published *Autobiography*. 'According to the circumstances of the time,' he
wrote, 'I have allotted myself so many pages a week. The
average number has been about 40. It has been placed

as low as 20, and has risen to 112. And as a page is an ambiguous term, my page has been made to contain 250 words.' For many years he made a practice of rising at 5.30 in the morning, spent half an hour reading over the previous day's work, and then wrote till 8.30, with his watch in front of him, aiming to produce 250 words every quarter of an hour, or 10,000 words per week, before going off to his day-job. The totals he actually achieved were meticulously recorded in a ledger. His work for the Post Office entailed a good deal of travelling by train, and instead of reading a book he would continue writing one of his own, using a pencil and a home-made writing board, to be transcribed later by his wife. When he made long journeys by sea, privately or on official business, sometimes as far as the West Indies, Australia and New Zealand, he always had the ship's carpenter construct a writing desk in his cabin and made good use of it.

What began as a self-imposed discipline became a habit, and eventually an addiction. Trollope simply couldn't stop writing. On 21 December 1880, when both his health and his popularity with the reading public were declining, he wrote to his elder son Harry, 'I finished on Thursday the novel I was writing, and on Friday I began another. Nothing really frightens me but enforced idleness. As long as I can write books, even though they be not published, I think I can be happy.' The novel Trollope started that week was entitled *The Fixed Period* and it was published in March 1882, the last year of his life. It received mixed, somewhat baffled reviews, and sold only 877 copies, making a loss for its publisher. It has not been any more popular with readers since then. The story is set in the

future, in 1980, on an imaginary antipodean island called
Britannula, and therefore lacks the subtle observation of
a recognisable social world for which Trollope's fiction is
cherished. It has a first-person narrator, a method he had
used before only in a few short stories, and then in a
style very like that of the urbane, sympathetic authorial
persona of the novels. The narrator of *The Fixed Period*,
in stark contrast, is earnest and humourless. Most disconcerting of all to Trollope *aficionados* is the novel's subject:
the effects of a law passed by the youthful Britannula
Assembly making euthanasia compulsory for everybody
between the age of sixty-seven and sixty-eight.

The Fixed Period has been largely ignored by those
who go to Trollope for a superior kind of comfort
reading, and dismissed as an aberrant minor work by
most critics and biographers. The article on him in the
New Oxford Dictionary of National Biography describes it
as 'worthy of mention only as being so much out of
Trollope's normal line'. Richard Mullen refers to 'this
unpleasant novel' as 'an oddity among his fiction' in his
biography of the novelist. John Sutherland also describes
it as 'the oddest item in all Trollope's fiction', in *The
Longman Companion to Victorian Fiction*. It is certainly
unique in Trollope's *oeuvre*, but also oddly relevant to
some of our own current social, economic and ethical
concerns. Due to advances in medicine and public health
Britain, like many other developed countries, has experienced a rapid rise in life expectancy in recent decades,
which means that more and more old and retired people
must be supported for longer and longer by the working
population, a situation that has been exacerbated by
the global credit crisis, with a consequent rise in

unemployment and a fall in the value of pension funds. At the same time there is increasing public controversy and private uncertainty about the legitimacy of assisted dying in certain circumstances. It is fascinating to see an astute Victorian mind exploring these issues through fiction.

In an introductory chapter, the narrator summarises the history of Britannula, an uninhabited island that was settled by a group of young emigrants from New Zealand, a country Trollope knew well. (He visited it in 1872 after spending a year in Australia where his younger son Fred was a sheep farmer, and wrote a book about his travels in both countries.) The colony of Britannula prospered and was granted independence by the British government. The narrator was the first Speaker of its Assembly, and at the time of writing is the country's President. He is a fervent advocate of the Fixed Period for rectifying 'two mistakes . . . made by mankind; first in allowing the world to be burdened with the continued maintenance of those whose cares should have been made to cease . . . and the second, in requiring those who remain to live a useless and painful life'. The aim of compulsory euthanasia is to convert death into a civic duty carried out with honour and dignity. For one year before their demise the old 'would be prepared for their departure, for the benefit of their country, surrounded by all the comforts to which, at their time of life, they would be susceptible, in a college maintained at the public expense; and each, as he drew nearer to the happy day, would be treated with still increasing honour'. It is a kind of utopian (or dystopian) version of the almshouses in *The Warden* (1855), Trollope's first successful novel. As to the expense of such a system, the narrator calculates that the savings which would accrue to the community by the elimination of its non-productive members would more than compensate. 'It would keep us out of debt, make for us our railways, render all our rivers navigable, construct our bridges, and leave us shortly the richest people on God's earth!' To the narrator's regret, however, this bold social experiment was thwarted before it could be put to the test, as he proceeds to relate.

He is called John Neverbend. Trollope liked to give some of his characters obtrusively symbolic names, wilfully violating the conventions of realism which he otherwise observed. (Henry James, who deplored the habit, said of Mr Quiverful, the father of fourteen children in *Barchester Towers*, 'We can believe in the name and we can believe in the children. But we cannot manage the combination.') A name like Neverbend is, however, appropriate in a fable of this kind. He is obsessed with his vision of benign euthanasia, and unable to empathise with the growing repugnance of the population to the idea as the time draws near to put it into practice. He is deeply offended when people refer to the method to be used ('certain veins should be opened while the departing one should, under the influence of morphine, be gently entranced within a warm bath') as 'murder' or 'execution'. He is shocked when his friend Gabriel Crasweller, who voted for the law when it was framed, shows signs of reluctance to be 'deposited' in the college, and vainly attempts to lie about his age.

Neverbend regards voluntary euthanasia as a more effective way to banish the fear of death than religion can
offer, and says to Crasweller: 'How best can we prepare
ourselves for the day which we know cannot be avoided?
That is the question which I have ever been asking
myself, and which I thought we had answered. Let us
turn the inevitable into that which shall in itself be
esteemed a glory to us . . . and you, oh my friend, have
ever been he whom it has been my greatest joy to
have had with me as the sharer of my aspirations.'
To which Crasweller replies flatly: 'But I am nine years
older than you.'

Although Neverbend is humourless, for the reader
there is humour, and also pathos, in the clash of his
high-flown rhetoric with the instinctive reactions of
others, including his own family. Neverbend is a zealot,
but not an insensitive one. As the opposition to the
Fixed Period grows, he actually begins 'to ask myself
whether I was in all respects sane in entertaining the
ideas which filled my mind', but steadies his resolution
by remembering the example of great men like Galileo
and Columbus whose radical ideas were mocked and
rejected in their own time.

Halfway through the book there is a long episode about
a cricket match played between Britannula and a touring
team from England, which gives Trollope an opportunity
to indulge his penchant for amusing names (e.g. Lord
Marylebone and Sir Kennington Oval) and to fantasise
about the future development of the game. In 1980 it
is played by teams of sixteen players, with mechanical

aids such as a 'steam bowler' and a 'catapult', which require the batsmen to wear wicker helmets and other protective clothing. The match is won by Britannula thanks to Neverbend's son's innings of 1,275 runs scored with his special 'spring-bat'. Trollope's speculations about other technological developments in the world of 1980 are sparse and rather timid. Transport in Britannula is still mainly horse-drawn, though Neverbend does have a steam tricycle capable of 25 m.p.h. Trollope is more prescient about communications: the British naval officers have a little device which works very like a mobile phone, and there is another which allows voice messages to be sent across oceans and emerge as text. But the novelist is not really interested in the science fiction possibilities of his story. The cricket match is introduced mainly to provide some humour and narrative excitement, and to foreshadow a second visitation from Britain – a gunboat sent to forestall the implementation of the Fixed Period law.

It arrives in Britannula's harbour just as Neverbend is conducting the sullenly compliant Crasweller to take up residence in the college. The officer in charge of the landing-party intervenes and forbids the President to proceed, invoking the threat of the gunboat's '250-ton swiveller'. Neverbend submits, vainly protesting against this exercise of brute force, and is informed that the island is to be made a Crown colony again, with a new governor to ensure that the law of the Fixed Period, unacceptable to the mother country, is repealed, while he himself must go into exile in England. The narrative we have been reading is in fact written on his voyage there.

★　　★　　★

To readers prepared to suspend their usual expectations of a Trollope novel, *The Fixed Period* is an absorbing, thought-provoking and entertaining tale. But what prompted Trollope to write it? According to his biographer H. John Hall he was inspired by a Jacobean play which he read in 1876, called *The Old Law*, by Massinger, Middleton and Rowley, in which the Duke of Epire promulgates a new law for the old, namely that every man who reaches the age of eighty and every woman who reaches the age of sixty will be put to death, 'cut off as fruitless to the republic, and law shall finish what nature linger'd at'. The law, however, turns out to be a device of the Duke's (similar to the plot of Shakespeare's *Measure for Measure*) to test the ethical character of his subjects: no one is executed, and those who hoped to benefit from the deaths of their elderly relatives are exposed and punished. Trollope's use of the basic idea is much more complex and challenging to interpretation. To most of its first reviewers *The Fixed Period* seemed like an extended joke in dubious taste. 'The joke is a somewhat grim one . . . too grim for light treatment,' said the *Spectator,* while the American *Nation* described it as 'an elaborate elephantine attempt at a joke by a person without any sense of humour'. But Hall records that when a friend referred to it as 'a grim jest' Trollope gripped him by the arm and exclaimed: 'It's all true – I mean every word of it.'

Because of its first-person narrative method the import of the novel remains ambiguous, but the remark shows that Trollope wished it to be taken seriously. As to why he wrote it, there are several clues in the biographical record. His letters at that time show him gloomily conscious of declining health. He had driven himself hard for years, and this lifestyle took its toll. By the late 1870s he was overweight and, according to Hall, had congested lungs, was short of breath, and probably suffering from high blood pressure. Two days before finishing *The Fixed Period* he wrote to a friend: 'I am now an old man, 66, and shall soon have come to the end of my tether.' In her biography Victoria Glendinning quotes a letter to his brother Tom written in 1881 or '82: 'the time has come upon me of which I have often spoken to you, in which I shall know that it were better I were dead', and Hall quotes words from another to the same correspondent that seem particularly significant: 'It will sometimes take a man more than 5 years to die.' Trollope was not afraid of death, and said so emphatically to his brother: 'There is nothing to fear in death – if you be wise. There is so much to fear in life, whether you be wise or foolish.' What he feared particularly was evidently the living death of senility and/or physical helplessness.

It is a fear that haunts our own era. The advances in medicine that prolong our active lives also make it more likely that we will succumb to various forms of dementia, or survive a stroke for years in a helpless and barely conscious state. It is a fear to which writers are perhaps particularly sensitive, partly because they have highly developed imaginations, and partly because, like Trollope, they may become addicted to the exercise of their craft and dread its withdrawal. It seems likely that he used the fable of *The Fixed Period* to explore and relieve his own anxiety by turning it into speculative fiction. Suppose a rational plan were devised to abolish the pains and problems of old age: what might it be like and how would it be received?

There are more than enough hints in the presentation of John Neverbend to prevent us from identifying his views with those of the implied author, but there is sympathy too. He is not a device of sustained and bitter irony like the proponent of Swift's *A Modest Proposal for preventing the Children of poor People in Ireland, from being a burden to their Parents or Country* (i.e., fatten the babies and sell them as meat). Neverbend argues his case sincerely, idealistically, and often eloquently. But the reprieved Crasweller argues effectively on the other side, affirming the human instinct to cling to life, and evoking the peculiar horror of awaiting a fixed date for one's death. Interestingly Neverbend boasts proudly to the British visitors that Britannula has abolished another institutionalised form of that suffering, 'the stain of capital punishment', which makes him seem inconsistent, but more humane. At the end he feels betrayed but also secretly relieved at being removed from his invidious position, and concedes that 'the Fixed Period, with all its advantages, was of such a nature that it must necessarily be postponed to an age prepared for it'. Our own age, with its memories of crimes committed in the twentieth century in the name of eugenics, is certainly not prepared to accept it. But as we struggle to reconcile the imperatives of sanctity of life and quality of life, Trollope's fable has resonances for us that it didn't have for his contemporaries.

Trollope's odd novel proved, in one respect, uncannily prophetic of his own demise. Neverbend recalls that when the Fixed Period law was being framed there was a long debate about the age at which it should be applied. Eventually this was fixed at sixty-seven and a half, though some flexibility was later allowed. At the beginning of November 1882, the year in which *The Fixed Period* was published, Trollope suffered a severe stroke, which paralysed his right side and deprived him of speech, but the fate he had feared was mercifully brief. He died in a nursing home on 6 December, five months short of his sixty-eighth birthday.

Postscript

When a shorter version of this essay was published in the *Guardian* on 15 December 2012, among the comments it received from readers on the newspaper's website was an interesting contribution from a lady identified as 'AggieH'. The theme of Trollope's novel, she wrote,

> . . . seems to be an issue for many generations. As I read, I was reminded of similar themes in short stories by Marcel Aymé in the early '40s and Kurt Vonnegut in the '60s. In Vonnegut's story of the future, the US population has been '*stabilized at forty million souls*'. The average age is 129. '*There were no prisons, no slums, no insane asylums, no cripples, no poverty, no wards. All diseases were conquered. So was old age. Death, barring accidents, was an adventure for volunteers.*' This 'utopian (or dystopian)' situation was achieved by law. '*The law said that no newborn child could survive unless the parents of the child could find someone*

who would volunteer to die.' To volunteer, you ring the Ethical Suicide Studios – known to all as 'the municipal gas chambers' – at the Federal Bureau of Termination. Its telephone number (and the story title) is 2BR02B.

It wasn't until I looked up Vonnegut's story that I realised this number when spoken is 'To be or nought to be'. It's a black-comic fable about population control: a man whose wife has just given birth to triplets and wants to keep them must find three 'volunteers'.

'Tickets on Time' by the French writer Marcel Aymé (1902–67) is a more whimsical fantasy, though its premise is closer to Trollope's. The story consists of extracts from the diary of a vain and ambitious Parisian writer, which begins:

> A ridiculous rumour is going round the neighbourhood about new restrictions. In order better to anticipate shortages and to guarantee improved productivity in the working portion of the population, the authorities are going to put unproductive consumers to death; unproductive meaning: older people, retirees, those with private income, the unemployed and other superfluous mouths. Deep down, I think this measure is quite fair.

The diarist changes his opinion when he discovers that writers and artists are classified among the less productive and useful members of the community. Nobody, however, is actually killed under this regulation. All are issued with tickets entitling them to a certain number of days of life per month, related to their value to society, and during the remaining days they cease to exist, by some means that is never explained but might be compared to the way digitalised information can be stored in the Cloud, deleted terrestrially, and later recovered. The diary entries over several months record the effects, both comic and serious, of this regime on personal and collective life. An elderly husband who was swallowed up into the ether when his monthly tickets ran out, suddenly rematerialises in his bed between his young wife and her lover. At first the new regulation seems to reduce extravagant consumption by the idle rich, but after a while a black market in tickets predictably evolves, workers selling some of their rations to the wealthy, so the inequalities of society are restored by market forces. Because death is temporary and virtual in this fable, less is at stake than in the other two texts, and it does not engage as directly with the ethical implications of euthanasia.

WRITING H.G. WELLS

E ARLY IN 2004, while waiting for the autumn publication of my novel about Henry James, *Author,
Author*, anxiously aware that Colm Tóibín was about to
publish his novel, *The Master*, on the same subject, I
occupied myself by writing the introduction to a Penguin
Classics edition of H.G. Wells's novel *Kipps*. Early in April
I made this note in my very occasional diary:

> Researching *Kipps* I came across in Wells's *Experi-
> ment in Autobiography* (1934) an interesting story
> of the ménage of Mr and Mrs Hubert Bland at
> Well Hall, Eltham. He was a Fabian, a philanderer
> who converted to Catholicism, she was E. Nesbit.
> Possible material for a novel like *Author, Author*
> here. Sex, politics, children's literature . . . How
> much has it been worked over?

Author, Author was a complete change of direction in
my work, and I had enjoyed researching and writing it
so much that I was receptive to this idea for another
book of the same kind. The potential novel I glimpsed
in those few pages of Wells's autobiography was one in
which his involvement with the Blands and the Fabian
Society in the early years of the twentieth century, and

the parallel development of his career with Edith Nesbit's at that time, would provide a structure similar to the relationship between Henry James and George Du Maurier in *Author, Author.* But I soon discovered from Julia Briggs's excellent biography, *A Woman of Passion: The Life of E. Nesbit* (1987) that Edith's interesting story began long before she met Wells, while his own continued long after they became estranged, so their relationship could be only one episode in a novel that was mainly about him. Meanwhile Colm Tóibín's novel about Henry James had appeared to great acclaim, which, as I had feared, affected the reception of *Author, Author* adversely when it was eventually published. If two books on the same subject appear in the same year, the second one invariably suffers. Unwilling to risk the same thing happening to my next book, I shelved the Wells project, and wrote a fictional novel set in the present day, *Deaf Sentence,* published in 2008; but when that was finished I couldn't resist going back to Wells.

The postponement was fortunate. I had written in my diary in April 2004: *'Possible material for a novel . . . How much has it been worked over?'* Little did I know, but it was probably being worked over at that very moment by A.S. Byatt, who five years later would publish a novel drawing on it. By that time I had started my novel about Wells, having spent a couple of years on research, and had written approximately 15,000 words. On 1 May 2009, I wrote in my occasional diary:

> I discovered in last weekend's newspapers that a major character in A.S. Byatt's new novel *The Children's Book* is inspired by and partly based on

E. Nesbit and her ménage, and that there is a sexual-predator character who resembles H.G. Wells. The Zeitgeist strikes again! I wondered despairingly if the Tóibín saga was going to repeat itself.

On further reflection I decided there was no real cause for concern. There was obviously much less overlap in the content of the two novels than in the case of *Author, Author* and *The Master*, and by the time mine was published there would be plenty of blue water between them. I decided to press on with my book without reading A.S. Byatt's, to avoid being influenced by it. If, however, I had started writing *A Man of Parts* straight after *Author, Author*, it might very well have appeared in the same year as *The Children's Book*.

Before I thought of writing a novel about Wells I already knew something about him from writing literary criticism about his work, but the more deeply I looked into the life the more astonishingly rich in human and historical interest it appeared. Beginning inauspiciously (he was the son of unsuccessful shopkeepers and apprenticed to the drapery trade at the age of fourteen) it stretched from 1866 to 1946, a period of global political turmoil, including two world wars in which he played a public role. The bibliography of his publications contains more than 2,000 items, including over a hundred books. He met and conversed with nearly every well-known statesman and writer of his time, and in his science fiction and speculative prose he foresaw the invention of, among other things, television, tanks, aerial warfare and the atom bomb. He made a strenuous effort to direct the Fabian Society towards his own idiosyncratic model of socialism (an updated version of Plato's *Republic*) nearly destroying the society in the process, and worked selflessly if vainly all his life for the cause of World Government. His *Outline of History*, published in 1920, was an ambitious attempt to 'teach the peoples of the world . . . that they are all engaged in a common work, that they have sprung from common origins, and all are contributing some special service to the general end'. It was a global bestseller.

'Thinking people who were born about the beginning of this century are in some sense Wells's own creation,' George Orwell wrote in 1941 ('Wells, Hitler and the World State'). Between the wars, however, his influence gradually declined along with the quality of his writing. The triumph of literary modernism in the 1920s made his fiction look old-fashioned, and the novels which have retained classic status, like *The Time Machine*, *The War of the Worlds*, *Tono-Bungay* and *The History of Mr Polly*, all belong to the first fifteen years of his long literary career. His mind remained fertile with new ideas – in the late 1930s, for instance, he proposed something he called the 'World Brain', an enormous bank of human knowledge stored on microfilm and distributed free to users by aeroplane, which needed only the invention of the microchip to resemble the internet – but the world paid diminishing attention to them. There was pathos in his own sense of this neglect in his last years, and in his deepening pessimism about the fate of the human race, epitomised in the title of his last book, *Mind at the End of Its Tether* (1945).

Wells was also a prophet of the sexual revolution of our own era. He believed in Free Love and practised it tirelessly. He was married twice to women he loved, but neither of whom satisfied him sexually, and had several long-term relationships and briefer affairs, mostly condoned by his second wife, Jane, and innumerable casual sexual encounters. Of particular interest because of the scandal they aroused were his relationships with three young women half his age: Rosamund Bland, the secretly adopted daughter of Edith and Hubert Bland, who was actually fathered by Bland on Edith's companion and housekeeper, Alice Hoatson; Amber Reeves, a brilliant Cambridge undergraduate, also the daughter of prominent Fabians; and Rebecca West, then at the very beginning of her distinguished literary career, whom he invited to his Essex country house in 1912 to discuss her witty demolition of his novel *Marriage* in the feminist journal *The Freewoman*, a meeting which led in due course to the birth of Anthony West on the first day of the First World War, and a stormy relationship that lasted for some ten years. Amber Reeves also became pregnant by Wells, by her own desire, with dramatic consequences. There were interesting liaisons with the writers Dorothy Richardson (who portrayed Wells in her novel sequence *Pilgrimage*), Violet Hunt and Elizabeth von Arnim. Then there was Moura, the Baroness Budberg, a Russian aristocrat who survived the Russian Revolution as the secretary and probably mistress of Maxim Gorky, whom Wells slept with one memorable night when staying in Gorky's flat in Petrograd in 1920, and met again after the death of Jane in 1927. Moura was the great love of his later life, and his acknowledged mistress, but she refused to marry or cohabit with him. Wells has the reputation of being a predatory seducer, especially of women much younger than himself; but in all the relationships I investigated, with the possible exception of the always inscrutable Moura, he was initially the pursued rather than the pursuer.

This is not to deny that he was sometimes reckless or selfish in his amorous adventures, just as he was capable of pronouncements on eugenics and race which are morally repugnant to enlightened minds today. The last chapter of *Anticipations* (1902) is particularly shocking, declaring (in a poorly constructed sentence) that

> . . . the men of the New Republic . . . will hold, I anticipate, that the small minority . . . afflicted with indisputably transmissible diseases, with transmissible mental disorders, with such incurable habits of mind as the craving for intoxication – exists only on sufferance, out of pity and patience, and on the understanding that they do not propagate; and I do not foresee any reason to suppose that they will hesitate to kill when that sufferance is abused.

And as regards 'those swarms of black, and brown, and dirty-white and yellow people . . . I take it that they will have to go . . . So far as they fail to develop sane, vigorous and distinctive personalities for the great world of the future, it is their portion to die out and disappear.'*

* In judging Wells it is worth noting that these and similar sentiments did not offend the leading lights of the Fabian Society, such

For these reasons I foresaw a danger in narrating the main story exclusively from Wells's point of view, and introduced a critical perspective through what might be called, by analogy with interior monologue, 'interior dialogue'. Just as young children sometimes handle their guilt or anxiety by engaging in conversation with an imaginary friend, so the aged Wells sometimes hears, and responds to, a voice which

> . . . articulates things he had forgotten or suppressed, things he is glad to remember and things he would rather not be reminded of, things he knows others say about him behind his back, and things people will probably say about him in the future after he is dead, in biographies and memoirs and perhaps even novels.

This device makes explicit the faults and follies of which Wells is often accused, while allowing him to defend himself. Most readers liked it, and a minority didn't, but without it I couldn't have written the novel. It is an invention on my part – I have no evidence that H.G. talked to himself in old age – but has some justification in that there is a similar dialogic element in several of his books, notably *The Anatomy of Frustration* (1936), where the controversial views of the principal character,

---

as George Bernard Shaw and Beatrice and Sidney Webb. On the contrary, reading *Anticipations* made them eager to recruit Wells to the society. A belief in eugenics as a solution to social problems was 'politically correct' in progressive circles in the early twentieth century.

plainly voicing H.G.'s opinions, are questioned sceptically by another character supposed to be the editor of the main text.

Representing sexual behaviour presents a special challenge for the writer of a biographical novel: how can you ascertain the facts about this most private and intimate aspect of a person's life? It wasn't a problem for me in the case of *Author, Author,* because I share the view of most of Henry James's biographers that he was a celibate bachelor who repressed or sublimated his inherent homosexual tendencies. Wells was, in this respect, as in others, the antithesis of James. Fortunately, for my purposes, he wrote a secret 'Postscript' to his 1934 autobiography about his sexual life, to be published after he and the women mentioned in it were dead, and it eventually appeared in 1984, edited by his son Gip, under the title *Wells in Love.* This gave me the essential facts about the major relationships in his life, and a large number of minor ones, as well as invaluable information about his sexual development in childhood and adolescence. It contains only hints of his proclivities as a lover, but these could be supplemented from other sources, especially his passionate letters to Rebecca West.

Like most people who have studied Wells's life and work, I came to the conclusion that he was riven with contradictions in principle and practice, but that he was also one of the most interesting and prodigiously talented figures in twentieth-century cultural history. The main problem for me was to find in a mass of fascinating material, including both his public and private life, a novel-shaped story, by which I mean one which has more cohesion and patterning than the faithful chronicle of a life can provide – 'life being all inclusion and confusion, and art being all discrimination and selection', as Henry James said in his Preface to *The Spoils of Poynton*, and as he also said in the Preface to *Roderick Hudson*:

> Really, universally, relations stop nowhere, and the exquisite problem of the artist is eternally but to draw, by a geometry of his own, the circle within which they shall happily appear to do so.

Very early in the gestation of *A Man of Parts* I saw it as a companion piece to *Author, Author*, in which James would be a minor character as Wells had been in the earlier novel; but Wells's life proved a greater challenge to fictional form than James's. When I abandoned the idea of making his relationship with Edith Nesbit and her family the hub of the story, it was not immediately obvious how I could draw an elegant circle round Wells's multitudinous interests and experiences. Gradually a solution evolved. There would be a frame story divided into two parts, very like the one in *Author, Author*, of Wells's last years, beginning in 1944 and ending with his death in 1946, set mainly in his Blitz-battered Regent's Park house, showing H.G. failing in health and morale, depressed by the negation of all his utopian hopes for mankind by the Second World War and the decline of his reputation as a writer, and bothered by the crisis in the marriage of Anthony, his son by Rebecca West, which was uncomfortably reminiscent of his own marital history. From this perspective he looks back at his life and asks himself whether it is a story of success or failure. Then between these two book-ends I would tell the story of the most interesting part of Wells's life, from childhood to the mid-1920s, following the sequence of relationships with the women who meant most to him: his wives Isabel and Jane, Rosamund Bland, Amber Reeves, Rebecca West and Moura, showing how they affected, fed into, disrupted, and threatened at times to destroy his career as a writer and public man. There were symmetries and correspondences in this series of women: two wives whom he loved but found sexually incompatible; two brilliant young women half his age, Amber and Rebecca, with whom he had children; two – Rosamund and Amber – who had younger admirers, rivals to H.G., whom they eventually married at almost exactly the same time. These parallels would help to give the novel pattern, that combination of repetition and variation which is present in all art, as well as illustrating an obsessive-compulsive streak in H.G.'s character.

In the title essay of my book *The Year of Henry James* (2006) I observed that the biographical novel, which uses fictional techniques to represent real lives, had become increasingly popular with writers and readers of literary fiction over the previous twenty years or so. The output of novels subsequently did nothing to make me revise this view: it seemed to me that at least 25 per cent of those I saw reviewed in newspapers and magazines were of this kind (and several of them were about Henry James). As the publication of *A Man of Parts* in the spring of 2011 drew near, this flourishing sub-genre figured in a more wide-ranging critical controversy in the media. William Skidelsky wrote an article in the *Observer* of 23 January under the heading, '*It's time to stop this obsession with works of art based on real events.*' He picked out *The King's Speech*, the hugely successful film about King George VI's struggle against his speech impediment, and Hilary Mantel's Booker Prize-winning novel *Wolf Hall*, about the life of Thomas Cromwell, as symptomatic of a general tendency in all the arts, and he cited a large number of other examples (including *The Children's Book* and my own forthcoming novel) as symptomatic of 'a shift in recent years away from works of pure imagination towards ones which combine fact and fiction'. This shift is undeniable, and is as evident in theatre, television drama, and even the visual arts, as in movies and novels. More contentious was Skidelsky's assertion that this tendency is a Bad Thing, because 'by being placed at the service of factual knowledge, creativity loses its justification and becomes devalued as a result'. In fact the works he cites are not 'at the service of factual knowledge' but build creatively on the basis of factual knowledge. A week later the historian Antony Beevor attacked the trend from a different direction, in a talk to the Royal Society of Literature on 'The Perils of Faction' which was published in a condensed form in the *Guardian Review* (19 February 2011). One of the chief perils he identified in historical and biographical novels was that 'when a novelist uses a major historical character, the reader has no idea what he or she has taken from recorded fact and what has been invented in their recreation of events'. This was to some extent true of most historical writing from antiquity to the Renaissance, but modern historiography is strictly evidence-based, making the biographical novel an object of suspicion to most historians and biographers.

I understand the concerns voiced by Skidelsky and Beevor, and sympathise with some of them. 'Faction', especially on film and television, media that are notoriously subject to cynical manipulation for commercial ends, can give a seriously distorted account of important historical events and personages, spreading in their audiences confusion and misapprehension which are not easily corrected. When applied to living people who are not in a position to protest, such productions can be hurtful and intrusive. The current wave of fact-based or fact-inspired narrative certainly carries with it a good deal of rubbish, some of it dangerous and meretricious rubbish, but because it is a genuine cultural phenomenon it is futile to oppose it on principle. These two writers object to 'faction' on opposite principles – Beevor because it is not wholly factual, and Skidelsky because it is not wholly imaginative. But the categories of narrative are not watertight: they leak into each other. Or, to change the metaphor, they belong to a spectrum which extends from the most starkly factual to the most fantastic, and in most examples of literary interest and value some elements of both fact and fiction are invariably present to some degree, from the Homeric epics and the stories of the Old Testament to the plays of Shakespeare and the prose fiction of the last three centuries. The modern novel as a literary form had its origins partly in the explosion of popular documentary or pseudo-documentary narrative in the late seventeenth century – confessions of reformed sinners, biographies of criminals, and reports of current events like plagues and wars. *Robinson Crusoe* (1719), arguably the first classic English novel, was a work of fiction disguised as a factual story, and so was Samuel Richardson's epistolary novel *Pamela, or Virtue Rewarded* (1740), the original model for many greater works of fiction, including his own *Clarissa*. The realist novel of the nineteenth century, in which the personal life is portrayed against a panoramic social background, evolved from the novels of Scott, whose fictional characters interact with historical personages and events. The Victorian novelists applied Scott's method in a modified form to the present or the recent past, connecting their own invented stories to real events, like the Battle of Waterloo in *Vanity Fair* or the Reform Bill in *Middlemarch*. James Joyce went to extraordinary pains to make his modernist masterpiece *Ulysses*, about the experiences of a number of Dubliners on a single day, 16 June 1904, correspond to historical and topographical fact in every detail.

The arguments of Skidelsky and Beevor depend on an oversimplified distinction between fact and fiction, but this is not to say that we should collapse the distinction altogether, as the American writer David Shields advocated in a book published in 2010 called *Reality Hunger: A manifesto*. It was a manifesto for precisely the development Skidelsky and Beevor deplored. Shields claimed that 'an artistic movement, albeit an organic and as-yet-unstated one, is forming', one of its key features being 'a blurring to the point of invisibility of any distinction between fiction and nonfiction: the lure and blur of the real'. Among Shields's favourite texts are Rebecca West's *Black*

Lamb and Grey Falcon, Simon Gray's *Smoking Diaries*, and the confessional prologue to Vonnegut's *Slaughterhouse Five*. 'Living as we do in a manufactured and artificial world,' he asserts, 'we yearn for the "real", semblances of the real.' There is, however, a difference between the real and a semblance of the real, and as readers we may legitimately object to being tricked into taking the latter for the former. That would apply, for instance, to publications that purport to be genuine memoirs by survivors of the Holocaust, but are exposed as works of fiction. The best-known example is Binjamin Wilkomirski's *Fragments* (1996) which won several prestigious prizes and awards before it was shown to be a fraud. However well-written they may be, such books muddy a vitally important historical record and their exposure as fictions encourages Holocaust-deniers. A less disturbing, but symptomatic, deception was James Frey's account of his recovery from drug and alcohol addiction, *A Million Little Pieces* (2003), which became a number one bestseller in America but was subsequently shown to be largely fictional, with punitive consequences for the author. Frey has since revealed that the book was rejected by seventeen publishers when he submitted it as a novel, but accepted when, with a little tweaking, it was repackaged as a memoir. Not surprisingly, since he is committed to work which 'blurs' the distinction between factual and fictional narrative, Shields was sympathetic to James Frey in his manifesto, and ridiculed the publisher's offer to refund purchasers of *A Million Little Pieces* if they supplied a sworn statement that they had 'bought it with the belief that it was a real memoir, or, in other words, that they felt bad having discovered they had accidentally read a novel'. As for himself, Shields says, 'I doubt very much that I'm the only person who's finding it more and more difficult to want to read or write novels.' Instead he is drawn to various forms of life writing: memoirs, journals, and something he calls 'the lyrical essay'.

Shields's manifesto is an exhilarating challenge to fresh thinking on these matters, but I don't share his disillusionment with the fictional novel, or his tolerance of the fraudulent nature of Frey's book. It's a matter of the implied contract between writer and reader. The words, 'a novel', on a title page are a clear declaration that the book is not purely historical, and that is crucial. But there are many different ways of combining fact and fiction, and each work must be judged on its own terms. Some bio-novels, for instance, put their historical characters into situations which they never actually experienced, or imagine encounters between historical characters who never met. Among the several novels about Henry James published after mine and Colm Tóibín's was *Lions at Lamb House* (2007), by Edwin Yoder, a Pulitzer Prize winner in the field of journalism, in which Henry James's brother William, the famous Harvard-based philosopher and psychologist, arranges for Sigmund Freud to visit Henry James, and submit him to a full-scale analysis to get to the bottom of his depression. Another was *What Alice Knew* (2010) by Paula Marantz Cohen, which has Henry, William and their invalid sister Alice collaborating to solve the mystery of Jack the Ripper's identity. Cynthia Ozick published a tale called *Dictation* in 2008 about a mischievous conspiracy between Henry James's and Joseph Conrad's secretaries. These books are of varying literary merit, but few readers are likely to be misled about their relation to reality.

There is another kind of bio-novel which gives historical characters fictional names, to signal that it is a work of imagination rather than history. Not surprisingly, this is a device of which Antony Beevor approves. An example is Gaynor Arnold's *Girl in a Blue Dress* (2007) in which Charles Dickens is recognisably portrayed as the hugely popular Victorian novelist 'Alfred Gibson', seen from the point of view of his wife 'Dorothea' (Catherine Dickens). The novel deals mainly with the couple's courtship and married life, which became increasingly unhappy and ended when Dickens fell in love with the actress Nellie Ternan and separated from Catherine. It ends with a long scene in which the question of whether Dickens's relationship with Nellie was sexual, which Dickens denied, and scholarly research has been unable to determine, is answered in an interview between the widowed Dorothea/Catherine and the character representing Nellie, a meeting for which there is no evidence and which is inherently unlikely. In this novel Alfred Gibson both is and is not Dickens. Dorothea both is and is not Catherine. We read with a kind of double vision, and when something occurs in the story that seems improbable or inconsistent with our knowledge of Dickens or Catherine we attribute it to their fictional avatars (in the cybernetic sense of that term). It is well done, but the constant readjustment of the reader's assumptions and expectations, which this convention requires, weakens the illusion of being immersed in the subjectivity of a historical person.

Having eventually read and enjoyed *The Children's Book*, I would not describe it as a biographical novel, but as a work of fiction built on a foundation of extensive historical research. There are resemblances between several of the characters and real people of the period which, for the reader who recognises them, enhance the authenticity of the novel's presentation of social history, but it would make perfect sense to a reader who did not. And there are always more important differences than resemblances, not least in the unlikeable character of the writer Herbert Methley whose controversial views on sex, and seductions of young women, associate him with Wells, but who is in most respects quite unlike H.G. Reinforcing this point, Wells is in fact one of several historical figures of the time who are referred to by name in the novel, and sometimes have walk-on parts, to give specificity to its historical context.

The kind of biographical novel I write is based on documented facts about historical persons, and does not invent any action or event with significant consequences for them, but uses fictional methods to explore and fill the gaps in our knowledge, which is primarily the subjective experience of the persons involved and their verbal interaction. It makes a different contract with the reader from those implied in the novels mentioned above. In *A Man of Parts* (as in *Author, Author*) I spelled it out in a prefatory note:

> Nearly everything that happens in this narrative is based on factual sources – 'based on' in the elastic sense that includes 'inferable from' and 'consistent with'. All the characters are portrayals of real people, and the relationships between them

were as described in these pages. Quotations from their books and other publications, speeches, and (with very few exceptions) letters, are their own words. But I have used a novelist's licence in representing what they thought, felt and said to each other, and I have imagined many circumstantial details which history omitted to record.

I quoted copiously from letters (with kind permission from the Wells Estate) for two reasons: firstly they give a vivid sense of what the writers were thinking and feeling at critical moments in their lives, and secondly they provide the reader with an occasional reality check on the narrative. The reader can be sure that events the letters refer to actually happened, and assess the consistency of other details in the novel with those facts. In a few places I was obliged to compose fictional letters or fragments of letters because the originals were unobtainable or because it seemed the most plausible means for information in my source material to be passed from one person to another, and I listed these in an appendix to the novel.

This is the most controversial kind of bio-novel because it comes closest to the territory of the historian and biographer, while being quite different in its aims and (apart from quoting from the subject's letters and publications) in methods. Applying techniques that evolved in the nineteenth- and twentieth-century novel, especially 'free indirect style', which fuses third-person narration with a character's inner voice, and alternating this kind of discourse with passages of dialogue, a bio-novel can convey a more immediate sense of a person's life *as lived* than biography, representing it through his or her consciousness, and in their verbal interaction with others. Biographers are confined by their rules to a more limited repertoire of narrative modes and stylistic effects. The voice of the biographer, writing well-formed prose, which may of course be eloquent and witty and a pleasure to read, reports the life mostly in a summary style – partly because there is usually so much life to get through, but mainly because so much circumstantial detail is irrecoverable. When it comes to explaining motivation for which there is no hard evidence, the biographer is forced to rely on formulae like, 'He may have thought . . .', 'Perhaps at this moment she was reminded . . .', etc. The biographer's voice remains inevitably dominant, while the novelist can present such speculative material in the inner voice of the character. To make this distinction is not to denigrate biography, but to argue that there is something to be gained by representing the lives of real, historical figures with the techniques of the novel. Hilary Mantel's comment on her treatment of the events leading up to the execution of Anne Boleyn, in *Bring Up the Bodies* (2012), her sequel to *Wolf Hall*, is apropos:

> Until now this story has not been told through [Thomas] Cromwell's eyes. What can a novelist add to the painstaking work of historians? Perhaps nothing; all she can do is create a parallel version, an intimate version, sneak you into rooms where the door is barred. The affair was a conspiracy. It did not, by its nature, leave those traces in the written record that historians need to understand it. Perhaps we can't understand it unless we feel it: the foetid atmosphere of Henry's court,

> seething with malice, superstition, fear. (*Guardian Review*, 3 October 2012)

The novelistic method involves inventing – or, as I would prefer to say, imagining – innumerable small units, and often larger ones, in the continuum of represented experience, but as long as these are compatible with the factual record, and the book is presented and read as a novel, not as history, no harm is done. Antony Beevor once remarked, no doubt tongue in cheek, that he wished writers of historical novels would print the bits they made up in bold type so the reader would know which they were. As he was well aware, this would completely negate the novelist's aim, which is to make the seams between the researched facts and the imaginative embodiment of them invisible to the reader, in order to create that illusion of intimate access to another's experience which the novel can achieve more effectively than any other narrative form. In fact, if *A Man of Parts* was printed as Beevor suggests, most of the text would be in bold. As any competent reader knows, a detailed description of a historical person's thoughts and feelings has to have been extrapolated from a few factual clues, since every individual's consciousness is largely concealed from others, and most dialogue in a biographical novel must be similarly worked up from a small amount of data since whole conversations, especially in the pre-electronic age, are very rarely recorded for posterity. An example may be useful at this point.

In July 1905 Wells spent a week at the Blands' spacious, ramshackle eighteenth-century house, Well Hall, having arrived there uninvited. In her biography of E. Nesbit, Julia Briggs describes the episode as follows:

> One afternoon towards the end of July H.G. turned up at Well Hall entirely without warning, carrying his valise and announcing, 'Ernest, I've come to stay.' He called Edith 'Ernest' because he had first supposed that the bare initial stood for a man's name, and what after all was more important than being Ernest? (Coincidentally, an early Bodleian cataloguer made the same assumption.) Edith was delighted with Wells's confident expectation of her hospitality, and immediately set about organizing entertainments in the form of tableaux and charades to celebrate his arrival and amuse him next day. These were based on titles of his books and he had to guess what they were: for *Love and Mr Lewisham*, Paul sat at a table, studiously reading, while little John, got up as Eros with a bow and arrow, shot at him. Wells stayed about a week, on this occasion, and while he was there completed the draft of his novel *In The Days Of The Comet*, writing in the garden as Edith herself did; it was not finally published till the following year.

As far as I recall, no biographer of Wells has thought this visit worth recording, perhaps because Wells himself does not mention it in the *Autobiography* or its Postscript, *Wells in Love*. The accounts of his and Jane's relationship with the Blands in those books are sarcastic in tone, coloured by the breach that occurred as a result of his

affair with Rosamund, and give little idea of how intimate
with each other the two families were for several years,
and how well Edith and H.G. got on together at that
time. The visit to Well Hall recorded by Julia Briggs in
her biography of Edith illustrates that very vividly, and
I made a note to include the episode in my novel
when I came across it. The corresponding passage in *A
Man of Parts* to the one quoted above is as follows:

He didn't wire in advance, but arrived uninvited
and unannounced at Well Hall, carrying his valise, and
said to Edith, when she came into the hall to see
who had called, 'Hallo, Ernest, I've come to stay for
a few days.' Her face lit up with a smile of pleasure.
'What a lovely surprise!' She took his hand and
kissed him on the cheek. 'You may be wondering
why – ' he began, but she waved away his explan-
ations. 'We're always delighted to see you, H.G. Stay
as long as you like.'

That evening the family put on charades based
on the titles of his books to amuse him and make
him feel at home. Paul sat at a table reading text
books and taking notes while young John, dressed
as Cupid, mimed taking shots at him with a bow
and arrow. He guessed 'Love and Mr Lewisham'
immediately but pretended to be puzzled for a while
to let the actors have their fun. An item performed
by Edith and the housekeeper-nanny Alice Hoatson
kept him guessing longer, till he exclaimed 'Anticipations!' Rosamund, now eighteen and a striking
young woman, with a pretty face and a buxom figure,
did 'The Sea Lady', miming the breast-stroke while

pursued around the room by Hubert Bland wielding
a shrimping net. He couldn't resist contributing to
the entertainment with a couple of improvisations
on Nesbit titles, which were warmly applauded. He
hadn't enjoyed anything so much for weeks, and
retired to bed in good spirits. 'You won't mind if
I'm not in evidence tomorrow until the afternoon,'
Edith said as she wished him a good night. 'I work
in the mornings.' 'So do I,' he said. 'That's perfect
then,' she said. (pp. 167–8)

This follows my source fairly closely, but there are obvious
differences which belong to the novel form. Briggs refers
to Wells as 'H.G.' which is how his family and close
friends always addressed him by this date. It's an index
of the familiarity that existed at this time between him
and the Blands. My passage begins: 'He didn't wire in
advance . . .' The third-person pronoun locates the narrative in Wells's consciousness, and is used throughout the
passage, and in fact throughout the novel, for this purpose.
It is usually possible to maintain this intimate effect with
some stylistic variation, by using the point-of-view character's given name, as I did frequently in *Author, Author*
– for example, '*Henry of course kept his opinion to himself.*'
Wells's Christian name was Herbert, and he was known
to his parents and relatives as 'Bertie'. Early on in planning the novel I decided it would be inappropriate to
use either of these names in passages focalised through
his consciousness, since in most scenes other characters
would not be using it to address him. On the other hand,
I couldn't use 'H.G.' as I had used 'Henry' in *Author,*
Author. That honorific abbreviation, bestowed upon him

in mature adulthood by others, he accepted and obviously liked, but he wouldn't *think* of himself as 'H.G.'. If I had begun the passage, 'H.G. didn't wire in advance' it would inevitably open up a gap between the narrator and the narrated for the reader, if only subliminally. Here and elsewhere, therefore, I was restricted to the third-person pronoun (and obliged to use some ingenuity to avoid possible confusion with antecedent references to characters of the same gender).

There is much more dialogue at the beginning of my passage than in Briggs's, and all of it except Wells's announcement of his arrival was imagined, to bring out the warmth of the relationship between Edith and H.G. This dramatises the biographer's summary statement that 'Edith was delighted with Wells's confident expectation of her hospitality'. The explanation of why he called her 'Ernest' is omitted because I introduced it earlier in the novel in describing their first meeting. The reference to the Bodleian cataloguer – a typical biographer's aside – is also omitted as irrelevant to the situation. The action is focalised through H.G.'s consciousness – most obviously when he pretends to be puzzled by the charade of *Love and Mr Lewisham*. Briggs describes only one charade; I invented two more to create an effect of 'scene' rather than summary, and made the enactment of *The Sea Lady* anticipate Bland's later inappropriate sexual interest in his daughter. Since I could not imagine the intensely competitive H.G. being a purely passive spectator, I made him reciprocate by miming some titles of Edith's books. The dialogue at the end of the passage dramatises the information that both hostess and guest worked on their writing during Wells's stay, and prepares for an extensive development of this fact in the following pages. For me this long visit of Wells was a very useful opportunity to show the two writers discussing their work-in-progress, and to inform or remind the reader of the content of *In The Days Of The Comet*, which was to have important consequences for Wells's career, and of Nesbit's masterpiece *The Railway Children*.

But why did Wells arrive at Well Hall without warning or an invitation? If the two homes were not connected by telephone at that date, why didn't he write or send a telegram asking if it would be convenient? And why did he want to go there to write anyway? These are not questions that Julia Briggs felt required to answer, but in a novel we expect actions to be motivated (if they are not, a mystery is created which must be resolved sooner or later). There is a hint of an explanation in the warm letter of thanks Wells wrote to Edith shortly after his return home, which Briggs reproduced in her next paragraph:

> The thing cannot be written! Jane I think must take on the task of describing the departure of a yellow, embittered and thoroughly damned man on one Thursday and his return on the next, pink . . . exultant . . . full of the most agreeable memories.

Julia Briggs does not mention that Wells's visit occurred soon after the death of his mother in June of that year – and there was no reason why she should have been aware of it, since she was writing a biography of Edith, not H.G. His mother was the dominant figure in his family in childhood and he had struggled against her will for years in the effort to escape the wage-slavery of the retail trade to which she had apprenticed him. He felt his subsequent success had never really reconciled them. He was upset by her death, and even more when shortly afterwards he read her private diary. According to Anthony West, in *H.G. Wells: Aspects of a Life* (1984), H.G. was deeply shaken by the unlikeable personality revealed in the diary, by evidence of his mother's growing dislike of his father, and the fact that she submitted to a third pregnancy in the hope of replacing her adored daughter Possy who died in childhood, only to be bitterly disappointed by the birth of H.G. This was the most likely cause of the 'embittered' mood which he hoped to throw off at Well Hall, but it didn't explain why he arrived there without first ascertaining that he would be welcome. To bridge this explanatory gap I wrote the following passage to precede his arrival.

He was upset by his mother's death, but unwilling to share these thoughts with Jane, or anyone else. He was irritable and restless in the weeks that followed the funeral, unable to get on with a new book he had started called *In The Days Of The Comet*. He bickered with Jane about household matters, and shouted angrily at his boys when they made too much noise in the garden outside his study window, making little Frank cry. 'What's the matter with you?' Jane asked. 'I need to get away,' he said. 'Where will you go?' 'I don't know,' he said. 'Maybe to the Reform. I could work in the library there.' He had been elected to this famous club, another feather in his cap, in March. He packed a few clothes and the manuscript of *In The Days Of The Comet* in a valise and set off for London, but on the journey the idea of staying at the Reform in the middle of July, when everybody he knew among the members, like Arnold Bennett and Henry James, would be in the country or abroad, did not appeal. He needed company, sympathetic company. He thought of Edith Bland. (p. 167)

This passage is mostly invention, but inferable from or consistent with the facts that are known about Wells's life at this time. It, or something like it, was essential to preserving the novelistic cohesion of the narrative.

Bio-fiction does not pretend to replace biography, but complements it, offering a different kind of interpretation of real lives. But by putting himself imaginatively inside the consciousness of a historical individual the novelist can sometimes contribute to interpreting biographical 'facts'. The episode of Wells's life that required me to use most imaginative reconstruction was his affair with Rosamund Bland. Few hard facts are known about it. It began probably at or near Dymchurch, in East Sussex, where the Blands had a holiday house, near the Wellses' home in Sandgate, in the summer of 1906, when Rosamund was a nubile, flirtatious young woman of nineteen, secretary of the newly formed group of young Fabians known as the Nursery, and very much under H.G.'s spell. According to Wells's own brief, slightly ashamed account in the Postscript, he 'never found any great charm in Rosamund', but 'she talked of love and how her father's attentions to her were becoming unfatherly', so he decided to protect her from incest by taking over her sexual education, encouraged by her natural mother Alice, 'who had a queer sort of liking for me'. Hubert Bland got wind of the affair and used it to blacken Wells's character among the senior Fabians later that year at a critical moment in his campaign to reform the society. Relations cooled between the two families but there was no permanent breach until, at some subsequent date, Wells and Rosamund were intercepted by Bland on Paddington Station in the act of going off together – 'for a dirty weekend in Paris' according to her sister-in-law's later testimony – and by some accounts the enraged father, an amateur boxer who used to spar with Bernard Shaw, thumped Wells before dragging his errant daughter home. It's an episode which no novelist could resist, and I had marked it for inclusion in my novel from an early stage.

Julia Briggs usefully pointed out that Wells may have planned to travel from Paddington to Plymouth to take one of the transatlantic liners across the Channel, a less conspicuous route than the shorter ones. She also believed the incident must have happened soon after 4 March 1908, because of a surviving letter from Rosamund to Jane Wells of that date, which begins:

Dear Mrs Wells,
    Of course you have an invitation to the Nursery lectures. I wouldn't think of sending you a ticket. It never occurred to me to write and ask you

because I thought you would understand that
you were to come if you wanted to. I'm so sorry you
aren't coming to our dance on the 20th. I thought
I might have had an opportunity of talking to you
a little bit.

Briggs asserted: 'it is virtually impossible that Jane Wells
would have been asked to a dance at Well Hall after
the event [at Paddington].' With this I had to agree,
but it created a serious problem for the cohesion of
my novel. As Briggs was aware, Wells began his affair
with Amber Reeves in the spring of 1908 – in fact
during her Easter vacation, when she was preparing for
her Tripos Part II examinations. It was the culmination
of a mutual attraction, cloaked by a kind of tutorial
relationship, which had developed at an accelerating
pace that year; one of the great passions of Wells's life,
and his most daring experiment in Free Love, which
lasted for nearly two years until very reluctantly he
agreed to end it. Why on earth would he go off on a
dirty weekend with a girl he never deeply cared for,
a few weeks before he and Amber became lovers? How
could I make this psychologically plausible, and not
utterly discreditable? I could not consult Julia Briggs
about the dates, because sadly she had died shortly
before I reached this stage in the composition of *A
Man of Parts*.

The problem baffled me, and blocked the progress
of my novel for some time, until I suddenly saw the
answer. Because the Blands had dancing when they
entertained large parties at Well Hall, Briggs had assumed
that 'our dance' in Rosamund's letter referred to such

an occasion, but it was much more likely that it referred
to a dance organised by the Fabian Nursery to which
Jane and H.G. had been invited as members of the
Executive. Rosamund was Secretary of the Nursery and
would naturally refer to it as 'our dance' in her letter. I
deduced that Jane had received from Rosamund a
Nursery flyer advertising the lectures and an invitation
to the dance, and that Jane had written to her asking if
she could attend the lectures but saying that she and
H.G. wouldn't be able to attend the dance. Rosamund
says in her letter that her sister Iris is staying with the
family at Well Hall, convalescing from a difficult child-
birth, and that she herself intends to go and stay with
Iris for two months when she returns home. It seems
very improbable that Edith and Hubert would host a
dance at such a juncture, and Briggs had to speculate,
without any evidence, that Rosamund changed her plans
to stay with Iris, in order to place the 'dirty weekend'
escapade between the writing of the letter and the
commencement of Wells's affair with Amber in the late
spring of that year.

Because the archive of the Fabian Nursery held at
the London School of Economics doesn't begin until
1910 it is impossible to verify that they held a dance on
20 March 1908, but Patricia Pugh's history of the Fabian
Society, *Educate, Agitate, Organize*, confirmed that the
Nursery did indeed organise dances in their early years,
which was good enough for me. I felt free to place the
Paddington episode in the early summer of 1907, a much
more plausible date for several other reasons. Rosamund's
letter to Jane nearly a year later has exactly the wistful
tone of someone who would like to heal a breach with

a former friend, regretting the missed opportunity 'of talking to you a little bit'.

Of course I could have ignored Julia Briggs's dating of the Paddington incident when I first encountered it, and placed it earlier in time – very few readers would have challenged me. But that would have been to break the rule I set myself: to respect the known facts. When the different documentary sources I consulted gave conflicting versions of the same event I favoured the one that seemed most plausible to me as a novelist. In the Postscript to his autobiography, Wells describes his third visit to Russia, undertaken primarily to interview Stalin, in 1934. He asked Moura, who had lived independently in Europe since she parted company with Gorky in 1928, but was now in a steady relationship with H.G., to accompany him. She refused, saying she dared not return to Russia for fear of being arrested, and that she had to visit her children in Estonia, where they arranged to meet on his return journey. He took his son Gip with him to Russia as companion instead of her. Visiting Gorky in his dacha outside Moscow Wells was stunned to discover that Moura, unknown to him and contrary to her own accounts of her movements, had stayed with Gorky three times in the past year, most recently only a week before his own visit. Wells felt betrayed and described vividly how he was plunged into paroxysms of jealous rage. He set off alone for Tallinn, Estonia, determined to confront Moura with her deception.

In *H.G. Wells: Aspects of a Life* Anthony West asserts, naming Gip as his source, that Wells and his son deduced

between them that Moura must be a spy working for
Russian intelligence, that she had been planted on him
at the very beginning of their relationship in 1920 and
had been reporting on him ever since. According to this
account, when Wells accused Moura of this in Tallinn
she admitted it, but told him that it was the only way
she survived the revolution and that 'as a biologist he
had to know that survival was the first law of life'. In
Anthony West's opinion, although Wells patched up
their relationship he never recovered from the disillusionment, and it was the underlying reason for the
misanthropy of his last years.

West's version of the episode was repeated by John
Gray in his book, *The Immortalisation Commission*, which
was published not long before *A Man of Parts,* and seri-
alised in the *Guardian Review* (8 January 2011). Without
Gray's end-note reference in his book, readers of that
piece would have assumed that it came from Wells's
Postscript, mentioned by Gray. It does not. Wells gives
a very detailed account there of his showdown with
Moura in Tallinn – it is the only dialogue scene in my
novel hardly a word of which I had to invent – and at
no point in it, or anywhere else, does he accuse Moura
of being a spy, only of being 'a liar and cheat'. Anthony
West's book is a mine of information but he is not
always reliable, and in this instance I have followed Wells's
account. If Anthony's version were true, why would
Wells give a false one in a work to be published after
he and Moura were dead? I find it hard to believe – and
I would have found it hard to render in my novel – that
he received Moura's frank admission in 1934 that she
was a Russian spy who had all along exploited him out

of self-interested motives, but that nevertheless he soon resumed a sexual relationship with her, begged her to marry him, and maintained that she was one of the few women he truly loved. Also her daughter Tania recalled in her memoir, *A Little of All These*, that Moura asked her in June 1936 to tell H.G. that she had been taken ill in Paris when in fact she had gone to Moscow to visit the terminally ill Gorky. Moura would surely not have bothered with this deception if two years earlier she had confessed to being a regular visitor to the USSR in the pay of OGPU.

It would be surprising if Wells, knowing something of Moura's life in revolutionary Russia, never suspected that she had been compromised into acting as an agent for Russian intelligence, but I took the view that he suppressed or was in denial of this as a possible explanation of her attachment to him, and in my novel it only surfaces towards the very end of his life. Admittedly, in this position it helps to make my narrative novel-shaped. Early in 1946, ill and confined to bed, he is troubled by doubts about Moura's past. Is she, as Anthony believes, a spy? Has she been reporting on him to Russian intelligence ever since they first met? He resolves to challenge her when she next visits him, and then changes his mind because he cannot face the consequence should she admit that it is true – the end of their friendship. When she next visits him, bringing a bunch of daffodils which she arranges in a vase, to his horror he hears himself saying without premeditation, "'Are you a spy, Moura?'" After a long pause, she replies:

'Aigee . . . That is a silly question. Shall I tell you why? Because if you ask that question of someone and she is not a spy she will say "No." But if she *is* a spy she will also say "No". So there is no point in asking that question.'

'No, of course not,' he says. 'Forget I ever asked it.'

'I have forgotten it already,' she says, with a smile, and removes the newspaper from the chair next to his bed to sit down beside him. 'Would you like me to read you something from the *Times*?'

'Yes, please,' he says. 'Read me the obituaries.'

We know that Moura visited Wells in his last illness, and that she read to him from newspapers, but this dialogue is all imagined. I make no apology for that because I think the scene reflects the ambiguities of the relationship between these two people without pretending to resolve them. And for me it made an aesthetically satisfying ending to the last scene in the novel in which H.G. appears as a living person.

ACKNOWLEDGEMENTS

All but one of these essays have been published before, sometimes under a different title, but most of them have been substantially revised and extended for this book, and in some cases are conflations of pieces originally published separately. 'The Late Graham Greene', 'The Rise and Fall and Rise and Fall of Kingsley Amis', 'A Tricky Undertaking: the Biography of Muriel Spark', 'Alan Bennett's Serial Autobiography', 'The Greene Man Within' and 'Terry Eagleton's Goodbye to All That' were originally published in the *New York Review of Books*. The essay on Amis incorporates an introduction to his novel *One Fat Englishman* published by Penguin in 2011. 'John Boorman's Quest' was originally published in the *Times Literary Supplement*. 'Simon Gray's Diaries', an extended version of an article which appeared first in the *Guardian Review*, was published in the *Critical Quarterly*. 'Frank Remembered – by a Kermodian' combines a contribution to *There Are Kermodians*, edited by Anthony Holden and Ursula Owen, presented to Frank Kermode in 1999 on his 80th birthday, with a review previously published in the *New York Review of Books*, and was first published in this form in the *Critical Quarterly*. 'Malcolm Bradbury: Writer and Friend' is a new essay which incorporates parts of several occasional pieces I have written about him since his death. The publication history of 'The Death of Diana' is explained in the prefatory note. 'Trollope's Fixed Period' and 'Writing H.G. Wells' are extended versions of articles that first appeared in the *Guardian Review*. I am grateful to the editors of these publications who commissioned the essays in their original form, or were receptive to my proposals to write them.

I am grateful to my agent Jonny Geller for his encouragement of the project; to my editor, Geoff Mulligan, for numerous suggested improvements of the text; to Jane Smiley for first drawing my attention to Trollope's *The Fixed Period*; to 'AggieH' for permission to include her contribution to the *Guardian* website about the theme of Trollope's novel; and as always to my wife Mary, for her comments on various drafts of these essays.

INDEX